# THE ActionScript™ 3.0
## MIGRATION GUIDE

### MAKING THE MOVE FROM ACTIONSCRIPT 2.0

KRIS HADLOCK

New
Riders

**The ActionScript 3.0 Migration Guide: Making the Move from ActionScript 2.0**
Kris Hadlock

**New Riders**
1249 Eighth Street
Berkeley, CA 94710
(510) 524-2178
Fax: (510) 524-2221

Find us on the Web at www.newriders.com
To report errors, please send a note to errata@peachpit.com
New Riders is an imprint of Peachpit, a division of Pearson Education
Copyright © 2009 by Kris Hadlock

**Editor:** Wendy Sharp
**Project Editor:** Myrna Vladic
**Technical Editor:** Joseph Balderson
**Copy Editor:** Jacqueline Aaron
**Proofreader:** Janine Baer
**Cover design:** Charlene Charles-Will
**Interior design:** Kim Scott and Charlene Charles-Will
**Compositor:** David Van Ness
**Indexer:** Julie Bess

ISBN-13: 978-0-321-55558-8
ISBN-10:   0-321-55558-9

9 8 7 6 5 4 3 2 1

Printed and bound in the United States of America

*I dedicate this book to all those who have been frustrated by Flash and want to take the next step into what I believe to be the first real sign of a complete ActionScript language.*

*I also dedicate this book to my wife, Lisa, who inadvertently introduced me to the world of Web design and development, and has stayed by my side through endless hours of neglect while I wrote this book.*

# Bio

**Kris Hadlock** has been a designer and developer since 1996. He is the founder of Studio Sedition (www.studiosedition.com), a Web design and development studio. He is also responsible for Distant Measures (www.distantmeasures.com), a Web application that creates complete and automated marketing campaigns. Kris is also a featured writer for the Web Reference Guide on peachpit.com and the author of *Ajax for Web Application Developers* (Sams Publishing, 2006). You can learn more about Kris on his Web site (www.krishadlock.com).

# Acknowledgements

Special thanks to Wendy Sharp; without her help this book would not be where it is today. Thanks also go to Jacqueline Aaron, copy editor; Joseph Balderson, tech reviewer; Janine Baer, proofreader; Myrna Vladic, production coordinator; David Van Ness, compositor; and Charlene Will and Kim Scott, interior design—for all their work on the editing and layout, and for the beautiful design.

# Contents

# Introduction

If you're an ActionScript developer with a computer science background, and you made the leap to ActionScript 3 when it was officially released in 2006, you don't need this book. But if you came to ActionScript through any of the myriad other routes Adobe Flash developers take—for example, from a background in design or animation—you might be like thousands of your peers, still writing your code with the familiar ActionScript 2.

Although the move from ActionScript 2 to ActionScript 3 is significant, the learning curve isn't as steep as it seems. AS3 provides a completely new structure for the language and requires a new virtual machine; but even with these changes, those who are familiar with AS2 should not have a hard time making the switch. *The ActionScript 3 Migration Guide* demystifies the differences by providing detailed comparisons of ActionScript 2 and 3. If you want to use all the powerful new features AS3 has to offer and you have a basic understanding of AS2, you are in the right place.

## Structure

Chapter 1 is essential to understanding the fundamental architecture difference in ActionScript 3 called the *display architecture*.

After Chapter 1, each chapter covers a common ActionScript functionality, comparing and contrasting the AS2 and AS3 ways to write the code that accomplishes that functionality.

This book does not cover everything there is to know about ActionScript 3. It is meant to help those familiar with ActionScript 2 make the transition to AS3 by learning the fundamental differences between the two languages.

## Code Format

Throughout the book you will be guided by tips that correspond to certain lines of code and explain the differences between the AS2 and AS3 versions. Code formatting, including color and spacing, is also used in the examples to show ActionScript as it truly appears in Adobe Flash. Here are a few tips to help you understand the code formatting:

Blue: Blue code identifies inherent ActionScript.

Green: Green code identifies strings used in ActionScript.

Black: Black code identifies custom code.

# The Display Architecture

THIS CHAPTER, ALTHOUGH SHORT, acts as a quick primer for under-standing future chapters. While later chapters compare and contrast ActionScript 2 and ActionScript 3, here you will learn the concepts behind the *display architecture*—a term that defines the hierarchy of visual items and their relationships to one another in ActionScript 3.

You will also learn how the architecture changes will affect your transition from ActionScript 2 to ActionScript 3.

# DisplayObject

The *display classes* are the classes behind every visual item in Adobe Flash, and the DisplayObject is the superclass of all display classes. All display classes inherit the DisplayObject properties, methods, and events.

As the superclass of the display architecture, the DisplayObject defines basic visual properties, methods, and events that all visual items have in common—for example, the x, y, width, and height properties. Visual items added to the stage within the Flash IDE, such as movie clip, button symbols, or even text fields, automatically inherit the common DisplayObject properties, methods, and events. Therefore, you can access the inherited properties, methods, and events without having to extend any ActionScript packages or classes.

**NOTE** Many properties that were once prefixed with an underscore, such as _x, _y, _height, and _width, have been updated to having no underscore, such as x, y, height, and width.

For example, if you create a movie clip symbol on the stage and name the movie clip instance myMC, you can access the inherited properties, methods, and events from the DisplayObject without importing or extending the actual DisplayObject class.

```
1    myMC.x = 100;
2    myMC.y = 100;
3    myMC.width = 50;
4    myMC.height = 50;
```

The code example is similar to what is possible with ActionScript 2; the difference is that all visual items are subclasses of the DisplayObject class.

The following page defines all of the classes that inherit the DisplayObject and represent the different types of visual items that exist in ActionScript 3.

# The Display Classes

**Table 1.1**  The Subclasses of the DisplayObject

| SUBCLASS | DESCRIPTION |
| --- | --- |
| AVM1Movie | Represents a legacy ActionScript 1 and 2 SWF that is loaded into an ActionScript 3 SWF. |
| Bitmap | Represents bitmap images that are loaded or dynamically created with ActionScript. |
| InteractiveObject | Represents visual objects that users can interact with using a keyboard or mouse. See Table 1.2 for the subclasses of the InteractiveObject. |
| MorphShape | Created when a shape tween is used. |
| Shape | Used by the ActionScript drawing API to create basic shapes. |
| StaticText | Represents static text fields. |
| Video | Used to display live streaming video. |

**Table 1.2**  The Subclasses of the InteractiveObject

| SUBCLASS | DESCRIPTION |
| --- | --- |
| DisplayObjectContainer | Represents a DisplayObject that contains DisplayObject children. See Table 1.3 for the subclasses of the DisplayObjectContainer. |
| SimpleButton | Used to create button instances. |
| TextField | Used to create text displays or text input. |

**Table 1.3**  The Subclasses of the DisplayObjectContainer

| SUBCLASS | DESCRIPTION |
| --- | --- |
| Loader | Used to load SWF files or the following image types: JPG, PNG, or GIF. |
| Sprite | Used to display graphics or contain children. MovieClip is the one and only subclass of Sprite. The only difference between a MovieClip and a Sprite is that a MovieClip contains a timeline. |
| Stage | Represents the Flash stage or the area where all visual items reside in Flash. |

# The Display List

In ActionScript 3, the *display list* represents visual items and the relationship they have to one another. The display list defines the complex relationships and hierarchy of visual items.

There are three main groups for objects represented in the display list: the Stage, DisplayObject, and DisplayObjectContainer. The Stage object is the base of the display list; therefore, all visual items have the same Stage in common. The DisplayObject represents all visual items, and the DisplayObjectContainer is a visual item—or a complex DisplayObject— that contains its own DisplayObject children.

Throughout this book you will learn ways in which the display list offers flexibility and control over visual items that were not possible in ActionScript 2. You will learn how to dynamically display an object in the display list, take control of a displayed object's depth, and gain an understanding of object relationships.

CHAPTER 2

# The Event Model

EVENT HANDLING IN ActionScript 2 and earlier can be confusing because events are handled in a number of conflicting ways. As a developer, you have the option of using event handlers left over from ActionScript 1, or new events from ActionScript 2. Some events are placed directly on button or movie-clip symbol instances, while others are not, and there are only partial implementations of the DOM event model. It's hard to decide which event model is the best option, and you are bound to run into debugging issues if you don't settle on a single method.

Luckily, you don't have to deal with multiple event-handling options any longer. ActionScript 3 has a new, streamlined event-handling model that is completely based on the DOM Level 3 Events Specification, meaning there are no more consistency issues.

This chapter examines the differences between the old and new ActionScript event-handling models, differences that are crucial to understanding AS3.

# Callback Functions

In ActionScript, callback functions are often triggered by an event in order to execute code when the event fires. For example, when using XML, a callback function can be triggered by an event that fires when an XML file is fully loaded and ready to be parsed. At this point, our callback function can read the XML file and run custom parsing routines.

ActionScript 2 and 3 differ in how they handle triggering callback functions. One way in which AS2 triggers callback functions is by using callback-function properties. In AS2 the event that fires when an XML file is fully loaded is a callback-function property. In AS3, callback-function properties do not exist; rather, all events are triggered based on event listeners.

## AS2: Callback Functions

In AS2, callback-function properties execute functions when particular events occur. Callback-function properties are simple to implement, but limited. Not all classes have callback-function properties, and the classes that do are not consistent, as the properties can be used in a number of ways.

The XML class's onLoad property lets you execute a custom callback function when an XML file has been loaded via an XML object instance. In order to use the onLoad property in a class, the Delegate must be used to properly scope the callback function. The following example shows how the onLoad property is used to execute a custom callback function named onXMLLoaded when an XML file is loaded into a class named Display.

| | | |
|---|---|---|
| Import Delegate to scope your callback function. | 1 | `import mx.utils.Delegate;` |
| | 2 | |
| | 3 | `class Display extends MovieClip` |
| A property is created to access the XML instance throughout the class. | 4 | `{` |
| | 5 | `    private var _xml:XML;` |
| | 6 | |
| | 7 | `    public function Display(Void)` |
| | 8 | `    {` |

<table>
</table>

The _xml property is used as an XML instance.

The onLoad callback-function property triggers onXMLLoaded through the Delegate.

```
9    this._xml = new XML();
10   this._xml.ignoreWhite = true;
11   this._xml.onLoad = Delegate.create(this, onXMLLoaded);
12   this._xml.load("path/file.xml");
13   }
14
15   public function onXMLLoaded(Void):Void
16   {
17       trace("XML has been loaded: "+ this._xml);
18   }
19 }
```

## AS3: Callback Functions

ActionScript 3 uses event listeners to trigger callback functions, thus eliminating the need for callback-function properties. For example, in AS3 the XML object does not have an onLoad callback-function property to trigger an event when an XML file is loaded. Instead, AS3 uses the URLLoader and URLRequest classes to load the XML file and the Event class to listen for the XML-file-loading process to complete. The Event class is the base class of all event objects in ActionScript 3, both native and custom. The Event class covers common events, such as the complete event. In this case the complete event determines when the external XML file is fully loaded.

**NOTE** The URLLoader and URLRequest **classes will be covered in Chapter 9.**

The Event class is passed as a default parameter to the callback function that an event invokes. The Event class has properties that can be accessed in the callback function. In the following example, the currentTarget property is used to retrieve the object that triggered the callback function. Having access to the Event object that triggered the callback is a benefit of the new event-handling model.

packages are covered in the next chapter.

URLLoader and URLRequest are used for loading.

```
1  package
2  {
3      import flash.display.*;
4      import flash.net.URLLoader;
5      import flash.net.URLRequest;
6      import flash.xml.*;
7      import flash.events.*;
8
9      public class Display extends MovieClip
10     {
11         public function Display()
12         {
13             var _loader:URLLoader = new URLLoader();
```

| | | |
|---|---|---|
| addEventListener and the Event class replace onLoad. | 14 | ```_loader.addEventListener(Event.COMPLETE,``` |
| | | ```onXMLLoaded);``` |
| | 15 | ```        _loader.load(new URLRequest("path/file.xml"));``` |
| | 16 | ```      }``` |
| onXMLLoaded is triggered when the XML file is loaded. | 17 | |
| | 18 | ```      public function onXMLLoaded(event:Event):void``` |
| | 19 | ```      {``` |
| currentTarget is the object that loaded the XML file while loader.data is the XML file. | 20 | ```      var loader:URLLoader = URLLoader(event.currentTarget);``` |
| | 21 | ```      var _xml:XML = new XML(loader.data);``` |
| | 22 | ```      trace("XML loaded, instance created: "+ _xml);``` |
| | 23 | ```      }``` |
| | 24 | ```    }``` |
| | 25 | ```}``` |

# UIEventDispatcher

The UIEventDispatcher class in ActionScript 2 is based on an incomplete implementation of the DOM event model, but is closely related to the new event model offered in ActionScript 3.

## AS2: UIEventDispatcher

The UIEventDispatcher class provides a means to register events on ActionScript 2 components. The UIEventDispatcher has numerous events to handle loading and unloading, and key and mouse presses. The UIEventDispatcher class also includes methods for adding and removing listeners, named addEventListener and removeEventListener.

This next example assumes that there is a button component with an instance name of myButton located on the stage. A generic object is instantiated to act as a listener, and a callback function is defined with the same name as the event defined in the addEventListener method.

| | | |
|---|---|---|
| A generic object is used as a listener object. | 1 | ```var listener:Object = new Object();``` |
| | 2 | ```listener.click = function(evt)``` |
| click is a callback function. | 3 | ```{``` |
| | 4 | ```    trace("myButton has been clicked");``` |
| | 5 | ```}``` |
| click is fired if myButton is clicked. | 6 | ```myButton.addEventListener("click", listener);``` |

To add to the event-handling confusion, the listener object is not even required, as callback functions can be triggered directly from the addEventListener method.

onClick is a callback function.

```
1   onClick = function(evt)
2   {
3       trace("My button has been clicked");
4   }
5   myButton.addEventListener("click", onClick);
```

onClick is fired if myButton is clicked.

## AS3: UIEventDispatcher

In ActionScript 3, the UIEventDispatcher does not exist, although you still add an event listener using the same addEventListener method call as you did in ActionScript 2. The difference with the AS3 addEventListener method is that instead of using a string parameter as the event type, you now use a custom event class to define the event type. AS3 offers multiple event classes to handle specific events that happen in your Flash movies. In the following example, the MouseEvent class is used to trigger a callback function when a button is clicked. The sample assumes that you have a myButton instance on the stage and are using the Display class as your document class.

MouseEvent is imported to later create a CLICK event.

The addEventListener takes a predefined MouseEvent constant.

The onClick method receives a MouseEvent object as a parameter since a mouse event triggered the method.

```
1   package
2   {
3       import flash.display.*;
4       import flash.events.MouseEvent;
5
6       public class Display extends MovieClip
7       {
8           public function Display()
9           {
10              myButton.addEventListener(MouseEvent.CLICK,
    onClick);
11          }
12
13          public function onClick(event:MouseEvent):void
14          {
15              trace("My button has been clicked");
16          }
17      }
18  }
```

As you probably noticed, another difference between the UIEventDispatcher and AS3's event model is that the new model doesn't need a listener object. All classes that inherit the DisplayObject or InteractiveObject classes inherit basic events.

# Event Dispatching

Event dispatching provides a way to separate your code, which allows your classes to not have to be completely aware of other classes in your project. For example, a class might react only to dispatched events to which it is listening or to which it is subscribed. Separating your code keeps packages and/or classes reusable, so that you can drop the code in any code base and the code will work without relying on other classes or packages.

**NOTE** Reusability speeds up development processes by reducing redundancy in code.

## AS2: Event Dispatching

The EventDispatcher class lets you add or remove event listeners so that your code can respond to events. The EventDispatcher also makes it possible for you to dispatch events from custom classes, although the process of setting up the dispatcher is not exactly straightforward.

Event dispatching requires importing the EventDispatcher class. The EventDispatcher class is needed to include the appropriate functions, fire the appropriate dispatching method, and initialize itself as an EventDispatcher. To use event dispatching in AS2, the dispatching class must first declare a dispatchEvent function, then an addEventListener function. Technically, only the dispatchEvent function is required; but no other class can subscribe without the addEventListener function, so the code is useless without both functions. Then the class needs to be initialized by the EventDispatcher; and finally, it can dispatch custom events.

The following code will dispatch a Load event and a LoadError event for a custom subclass of the XML class called SuperXML. The purpose of SuperXML is to simplify the code required to create XML object instances and have more control over the events that the instances dispatch.

EventDispatcher is imported to enable us to dispatch events.

dispatchEvent dispatches events and addEventListener provides a way to listen to dispatched events.

To dispatch events, the class must be initialized by the EventDispatcher.

```
1   import mx.events.EventDispatcher;
2
3   class SuperXML extends XML
4   {
5       public var dispatchEvent:Function;
6       public var addEventListener:Function;
7       public var _url:String;
8
9       public function SuperXML(Void)
10      {
11      super();
12          EventDispatcher.initialize(this);
13          this.ignoreWhite = true;
```

```
14          this.xmlDecl = '<?xml version="1.0" ?>';
15      }
16
17      public function load(path:String):Void
18      {
19          this._url = path;
20          super.load(path);
21      }
22
23      private function onLoad(success:Boolean):Void
24      {
25          if(success)
26          {
27              dispatchEvent({type:"Load", xml:this});
28          }
29          else
30          {
31              dispatchEvent({type:"LoadError", url:this});
32          }
33      }
34 }
```

onLoad determines whether an XML file successfully loaded and dispatches the appropriate event.

In order to subscribe to an event from the SuperXML class, you need to start by instantiating the SuperXML class and loading an XML file. Since the SuperXML class is dispatching a Load and a LoadError event, you can subscribe to both and create custom methods to handle what happens in each event.

```
1  import mx.utils.Delegate;
2  import SuperXML;
3
4  class Display extends MovieClip
5  {
6      public function Display(Void)
7      {
8          var xml:SuperXML = new SuperXML();
9          xml.load("path/file.xml");
10         xml.addEventListener("Load", Delegate.create(this,
   onXMLLoaded));
11         xml.addEventListener("LoadError", Delegate.
   create(this, onXMLError));
12      }
13
```

SuperXML eliminates the need for ignoreWhite, or to set an xmlDecl, and provides a way to store the file path.

To properly scope events to class methods from SuperXML, Delegate must be used.

```
14    public function onXMLLoaded(xml:XML):Void
15    {
16        trace("XML has been loaded: "+ xml);
17    }
18
19    public function onXMLError(xml:XML):Void
20    {
21        trace("There has been an error loading the xml");
22    }
23 }
```

# AS3: Event Dispatching

As mentioned earlier, there are a number of native event classes in ActionScript 3. Each native event class has its own set of constants that define the values of specific events that can occur within the specified event class.

There is an actual native class by the name of Event, which contains basic event types that occur in Flash, but sometimes the types offered are not enough for custom classes that need to dispatch their own events. For this very reason, in AS3 it is possible to create custom event objects by inheriting the Event class, just as native ActionScript event classes do.

Let's say you want to dispatch a custom event when a start button is pressed in a video player. The start button is a property in a class called VideoDisplay, and other classes can subscribe to the start button in order to be notified when the button is pressed. Let's start by creating a custom event class, named VideoDisplayEvent.

The Event class needs to be imported to inherit it.

START is a custom event type that listeners can subscribe to.

The VideoDisplayEvent uses the superclass to fire the event.

```
1  package
2  {
3      import flash.events.Event;
4
5      class VideoDisplayEvent extends Event
6      {
7          public static const START:String = "start";
8
9          public function VideoDisplayEvent(type:String)
10         {
11             super(type, true);
12         }
13
```

```
14          public override function clone():Event
15      {
16          return new VideoDisplayEvent(type);
17      }
18      }
19  }
```

When the VideoDisplayEvent class is created, the VideoDisplay class can start dispatching events. The START event type will notify listeners when the start button is pressed in the video display. First, the VideoDisplayEvent needs to be imported. Then a dispatchEvent method can be added to the start button's click event in order to fire a new VideoDisplayEvent. The VideoDisplayEvent takes a property defining what type of event it is dispatching. In this case, the event is start, represented by the START constant in the VideoDisplayEvent class.

MouseEvent is used when the start button is clicked.

Import VideoDisplayEvent for later use of events.

```
1   package
2   {
3       import flash.display.*;
4       import flash.events.MouseEvent;
5       import VideoDisplayEvent;
6
7       public class VideoDisplay extends MovieClip
8       {
9           public function VideoDisplay()
10          {
11              startButton.addEventListener(MouseEvent.CLICK,
    onStart);
12          }
13
14          public function onStart(event:MouseEvent):void
15          {
16              this.dispatchEvent(new VideoDisplayEvent
    (VideoDisplayEvent.START));
17          }
18      }
19  }
```

onStart is triggered when the start button is clicked. A subscribing class can listen to the START event that is dispatched.

Other classes can subscribe to the events dispatched by the VideoDisplay. The following Display class is a document class that imports both the VideoDisplay and VideoDisplayEvent classes. The VideoDisplay class is attached to a movie clip in the Flash library so that the Display class has the ability to attach VideoDisplay instances to the stage. Since the

VideoDisplay class definition contains an event dispatcher, VideoDisplay instances can subscribe to the START event type by adding an event listener. At this time, a custom class method can be the callback function when the START event is triggered, as in the following example with the onVideoStart method. Now that a custom event exists, you can even type the event parameter as VideoDisplayEvent in the callback function.

VideoDisplay and VideoDisplayEvent classes are imported.

A new VideoDisplay instance is created and added to the stage.

When the VideoDisplay dispatches the START event, the onVideoStart method calls can be triggered to execute additional code.

```
1   package
2   {
3       import flash.display.*;
4       import VideoDisplay;
5       import VideoDisplayEvent;
6
7       public class Display extends MovieClip
8       {
9           public function Display()
10          {
11              var vd:VideoDisplay = VideoDisplay
    (addChild(new VideoDisplay()));
12              vd.addEventListener(VideoDisplayEvent.START,
    onVideoStart);
13          }
14
15          public function onVideoStart(event:VideoDisplayEvent)
    :void
16          {
17              trace("The video display start button has been
    clicked");
18          }
19      }
20  }
```

CHAPTER 3

# Packages and Classes

PACKAGES AND CLASSES are fundamental to object-oriented languages, and this chapter is all about learning how to create packages, reap the benefits of class attributes, and learn new ways to assign classes. You'll also discover the differences between the ways ActionScript 2 and ActionScript 3 handle a multitude of object-oriented concepts. And you'll attempt to do it all without a headache!

# Packages

Packages are standard in object-oriented programming languages. A package acts as a sort of code filing system, where the package is a folder and the classes are the documents within. On your computer, a package is used to group similar classes. Packages organize your code into groups based on similarity and/or functionality.

## AS2: Packages

In ActionScript 2, the syntax for package definitions doesn't formally exist. You can use a base package as part of a class path and create the package on your file system, but it's strictly for organizational purposes. True package definitions let you limit access to your class definitions. In AS2 you can't use packages to set access limits on your class definitions; any class can import and use any other class regardless of what package it's in.

It is a good practice, however, to create a base package. A base package is used to group similar packages—for example, packages that belong to a particular company or organization.

```
class com.yourcompanyname
```

If your base package is based on your company name, the first part would start with your Web domain. When finished, a base package often looks like your Web address written backward.

The packages you choose to create within your base package can be anything that makes organizational sense. For example, if I had a group of utility classes, I could create a folder named utilities and add it to the base package.

```
class com.yourcompanyname.utilities.StringUtils
```

## AS3: Packages

In ActionScript 3, you must use the package definition keyword when defining a class. Instead of adding the class path to the class definition, you now add it after the package definition keyword. Within the package definition, you identify the class keyword followed by the class name.

com.yourcompanyname
.utilities is the full
path of the utilities package. utilities will contain classes that perform common tasks, including StringUtils, used for general string manipulation.

```
1  package com.yourcompanyname.utilities
2  {
3      class StringUtils
4      {
5      }
6  }
```

If your class does not have a class path, simply wrap the class in a package definition.

```
1   package
2   {
3       class StringUtils
4       {
5       }
6   }
```

Note that Flash allows AS3 class paths to be verified, although not AS2 class paths.

**Figure 3.1**  *Verifying class paths in Flash when using AS3.*

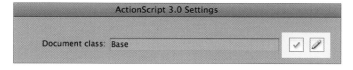

**Figure 3.2**  *You are alerted with a warning if Flash cannot find the class.*

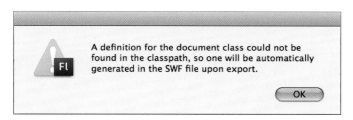

In ActionScript 3, packages are still used to organize your code, but they are now true package definitions, which allow you to define whether or not the classes within the package are accessible by external packages, based on the class attributes.

# Class Attributes

The benefit of using class attributes is that you can define the accessibility of a class to other classes and/or packages, and determine whether a class can be inherited and whether properties or methods can be added to the class at run time. There are a number of class attributes that can set privileges for your classes. The class attribute that you use can determine whether your class is accessible globally or only within the package in which it resides, whether it can be inherited (extended or sub-classed), or if properties can be added to the class during run time.

## AS2: Class Attributes

ActionScript 2 doesn't include class attributes that limit access. In AS2 all classes are public, which means classes can be accessed from any other class within the code base of a project. Let's take the StringUtils class as an example.

StringUtils is public by default and cannot be changed. Any class within a project that contains StringUtils will have access to it.

Truncate takes a string and shortens it to a specified length, then adds ellipses to the end to identify that the string has been shortened.

```
 1  class com.yourcompanyname.utilities.StringUtils
 2  {
 3      public static function Truncate(_string:String,
    _length:Number):String
 4      {
 5          if(_string.length > _length)
 6          {
 7              _string = _string.substring(0, _length) + "...";
 8          }
 9          return _string;
10      }
11  }
```

Any class, within any package of a particular project, can access the StringUtils class since all classes are public in AS2. Therefore the following code would work without any compiler errors and the trace would output the result of the Truncate method.

The trace of the Truncate method would result in: This...

```
 1  import com.yourcompanyname.utilities.StringUtils;
 2
 3  class com.yourcompanyname.view.Display
 4  {
 5      public function Display(Void)
 6      {
 7          trace(StringUtils.Truncate("This could be a very long
    string.", 4));
 8      }
 9
10  }
```

## AS3: Class Attributes

If you updated the StringUtils class to ActionScript 3 without using a class attribute, the previous code example would produce a compiler error; but if you typed the StringUtils class as public, it would pass with flying colors.

StringUtils needs to be typed with a `public` attribute to produce the same results as in ActionScript 2. If `StringUtils` is not typed with the `public` attribute, it will be considered `internal` and accessible only to classes within the utilities package.

```
1  package com.yourcompanyname.utilities
2  {
3      public class StringUtils
4      {
5      }
6  }
```

The AS2 code example would produce an error because `public` is no longer the default class attribute; ActionScript 3 defaults to the `internal` class attribute. The `internal` class attribute does more than create compiler errors in ActionScript 3 code, though; it actually provides privacy to your classes by giving access only to other classes that are within the same package. The following code is an example of an `internal` StringUtils class.

Typing the `StringUtils` class as `internal` makes it inaccessible to packages outside the `utilities` package.

```
1  package com.yourcompanyname.utilities
2  {
3      internal class StringUtils
4      {
5          public static function Truncate(_string:String,
   _length:Number):String
6          {
7              if(_string.length > _length)
8              {
9                  _string = _string.substring(0, _length)
   + "...";
10             }
11             return _string;
12         }
13     }
14 }
```

As an `internal` class, StringUtils is accessible only from other classes within the utilities package. In fact, it is not even necessary to import StringUtils if the accessing class is within the same package as the `internal` class, in this case the utilities package.

UtilityDelegate could be used to access the `internal` classes within the `utilities` package.

The trace of the `Truncate` method would result in This...

```
1  package com.yourcompanyname.utilities
2  {
3      public class UtilityDelegate
4      {
5          public function UtilityDelegate()
6          {
7              trace(StringUtils.Truncate("This could be a very
   long string.", 5));
```

```
8              }
9
10         }
11 }
```

In addition to `internal`, the `final` attribute is also new to ActionScript 3. Classes using the `final` attribute cannot be inherited, which can be useful in configuration classes, or any class that strictly contains constants that will not be changed. For example, if you have a configuration class with information that you do not want altered, you would not want it to be inherited, especially if the code base offered an API that let other developers access your code. In addition to preventing inheritance, the `final` attribute is paired with a `public` or `internal` attribute for an extra level of control. Here is an example of a `final`, `public` configuration class, which uses the `const` keyword to define the property as a constant.

**NOTE** You will learn more about the `const` keyword in the next chapter.

The Configuration class is `final`, so it cannot be inherited, but it's still globally accessible because of the `public class` attribute.

Other important constants could be defined here.

```
1 package com.yourcompanyname.constants
2 {
3     final public class Configuration
4     {
5         public static const MODE:String = "runtime";
6     }
7 }
```

# Class Assignment

When I first learned ActionScript 2, I quickly picked up the code, but it took me a while to understand how to assign a class to a Flash movie. Assigning a class to a movie is unique to Flash, as other languages don't have a concept of movies.

## AS2: Class Assignment

In ActionScript 2, a linkage name or identifier is how you assign your classes to a symbol in the Flash movie, such as a movie clip or button. You create this link through the library window, by right-clicking or control-clicking a library item and choosing the Linkage option. Once the Linkage Properties dialog is open, you choose Export for ActionScript and define a class by entering the full class path, which includes the class name, in the class text field.

**Figure 3.3** *The Linkage Properties dialog lets you assign classes to symbols in your Flash movie.*

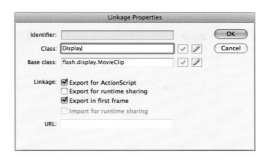

To tie a class to a Flash movie, the class must be linked to a symbol in the library. There is no other way to link a class and a movie with ActionScript 2.

## AS3: Class Assignment

You can still assign classes using linkage, and in many cases you should, but in ActionScript 3 you can also attach a document class when creating an access or movie class. (If it had been possible to create a document class when I learned ActionScript 2, it would have saved me a few headaches.) Assigning a document class helps separate your main access class from supporting classes. You set the document class simply by entering the name of the class in the document-class text field that is located in the Properties window.

**Figure 3.4** *In ActionScript 3 you can assign a class to the Flash movie.*

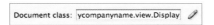

A document class is associated with the SWF file as a root level container class. The document class needs to inherit the `DisplayObject` class because the SWF file and stage are display objects. If the `Display` class from the previous chapter was used as our document class, it would need to import a `DisplayObject` class in order to inherit a `DisplayObject`. The following code is an example of the `Display` class inheriting the `Sprite` as a `DisplayObject`.

To inherit the `Sprite` class, the `display` package is imported. Importing the entire `display` package provides access to all the classes within the package and does not add extra weight to the project. Only the classes that you use are exported with the Flash movie.

```
 1  package com.yourcompanyname.view
 2  {
 3      import flash.display.*;
 4      public class Display extends Sprite
 5      {
 6          public function Display()
 7          {
 8              super();
 9          }
10      }
11  }
```

# Import

You often need to import classes or entire class packages into your scripts in order to use them. AS2 and AS3 have different requirements for importing classes.

## AS2: Import

ActionScript 2 requires you to import custom classes in order to use them unless you use the fully qualified class name. However, AS2 doesn't require you to import inherent Flash classes that directly inherit `Object,` although it is a best practice to do so. All the classes listed in the AS2 help documentation are inherent Flash classes that don't need to be imported. You don't have to import these classes even when inheriting or typing class properties, method parameters, or return values.

The following `Display` class is error free in AS2, but it will not pass the compiler in ActionScript 3 because the `MovieClip` class is not imported. In this case the `MovieClip` class can be extended, and our `item` property can be typed as a `MovieClip` without actually importing the `MovieClip` class.

> It's not necessary to import the `MovieClip` class in order to inherit or type a class property.

```
1   class com.yourcompanyname.view.Display extends MovieClip
2   {
3       public var item:MovieClip;
4       public function Display(Void)
5       {
6           super();
7       }
8   }
```

## AS3: Import

ActionScript 3 has considerably more stringent import requirements. You must import a class any time you want to use it—unless, of course, you write the full path to the class each time you reference it.

While it may seem like a hassle at first to write with all the new requirements in AS3, it makes debugging much easier and can actually force you to write less buggy code. AS2 may seem quicker to type, but it's really not once you get the hang of AS3; in fact, it's far more difficult to figure out what's going on when something goes wrong and your code is loosely typed.

In order for our `Display` class to use `MovieClip` as a `super` class, class property, or the return value of a method, it must `import` the `MovieClip` class. If the `MovieClip` class is not imported, the compiler will throw an error. This holds true for any inherited class or class used as a property or method type.

The `flash.display` package must be imported in order to inherit the `MovieClip` class.

**NOTE** When importing an entire class package, only the classes that are used within your script are exported with your Flash movie.

```
 1  package com.yourcompanyname.view
 2  {
 3      import flash.display.*;
 4      public class Display extends MovieClip
 5      {
 6          public function Display()
 7          {
 8              super();
 9          }
10      }
11  }
```

# Constructors

Constructor functions share the same name as the class that defines them. When a new instance of a class is created, the constructor function for that class is commonly used to initialize specific class properties or methods. For example, the `super` statement is commonly used in the constructor function to invoke the `super` class constructor.

You can also use the constructor function to create a singleton pattern, basically creating a class that restricts itself to a single instance and guaranteeing that any classes that use it will receive a consistent response, based on its stored values. The constructor function sets the single instance limit, although this is accomplished differently in AS3 than in AS2.

## AS2: Super

The `super` statement can be used to invoke the `super` class constructor in ActionScript 2. For example, if you create a class that inherits the `MovieClip` class, you can use the `super` statement to call the `MovieClip` classes' constructor function, and any code within the `MovieClip` classes' constructor function will be executed. Although it can be useful, ActionScript 2 limits the use of the `super` statement, as it has to be the first line of code in the constructor function. This limits the way the `super` function is implemented, as it forces the `super` class constructor to run before the subclass constructor.

```
1   class com.yourcompanyname.view.Display extends MovieClip
2   {
3       public function Display(Void)
4       {
5           super();
6       }
7   }
```

Constructor code needs to be added after the super statement. Constructor code commonly consists of initializing class properties and methods.

## AS3: Super

In ActionScript 3 the super statement is limitless and free, as you can call super from anywhere in the subclasses' constructor body. This allows the subclass constructor to run code before it invokes and executes any code that may be defined in the super class constructor. The possibility of adding code before the super statement is useful because you may want to execute class properties and methods before invoking the super class constructor.

```
1   package com.yourcompanyname.view
2   {
3       import flash.display.*;
4       public class Display extends MovieClip
5       {
6           public function Display()
7           {
8               super();
9           }
10      }
11  }
```

**NOTE** In ActionScript 3, constructor code can now be added before the super statement. In this example, any properties or methods in the Display class can be initialized before executing the properties or methods of the MovieClip class.

## AS2: Singleton Pattern

The singleton pattern can be crucial in solving situational programming problems. For example, I once worked for an e-learning company and had one particular project that used the Tween object for dozens of animations. Because the course was screen based, if an animation was not complete at the time a user advanced to the next screen, the animation would continue to run in later screens, creating an animation nightmare.

I created a class called the TweenManager to control every animation that was created. The TweenManager stored an array of Tween objects until they were forcefully removed, allowing use of the singleton pattern to control the same object through the entire course. This meant that any object in the course had access to adding and removing tweens. Therefore, when a user advanced to the next screen, all existing Tween objects were removed and the nightmare was over.

It's common in ActionScript 2 to use a private constructor to help create a singleton pattern. A private constructor prevents a class from being instantiated externally, thus forcing use of the singleton pattern. Instead the class is instantiated through a static method, such as the one in the code below called Instance. The Instance method ensures that the class has only been instantiated one time when an external object accesses it, by checking to see if a class property called _instance is null.

Imported to create Tween instances.

_instance is accessed through the Instance method and is typed as a TweenManager.

tweenArray stores Tween instances created by TweenManager.

The private constructor restricts TweenManager from being instantiated externally, but provides access for internal instantiation.

Instance is the only way to access the TweenManager instance, its public properties and methods. Instance creates one instance of the TweenManager if one has not been created, then returns the instance.

CreateTween takes the same parameters as the Tween object, creates Tween instances, and stores them in tweenArray.

```
1   import mx.transitions.Tween;
2   import mx.transitions.easing.*;
3
4   class com.krishadlock.utils.TweenManager
5   {
6       private static var _instance:TweenManager;
7       public var tweenArray:Array;
8
9       private function TweenManager()
10      {
11          this.tweenArray = new Array();
12      }
13
14      public static function Instance(Void):TweenManager
15      {
16          if(TweenManager._instance == null)
17          {
18              TweenManager._instance = new TweenManager();
19          }
20          return TweenManager._instance;
21      }
22
23      public function CreateTween(mc:MovieClip, _property:String,
    _method:Function, _start:Number, _end:Number, _speed:Number,
    _type:Boolean):Tween
24      {
25          this.tweenArray.push( new Tween(mc, _property, _
    method, _start, _end, _speed, _type) );
26          return this.tweenArray[ this.tweenArray.length-1 ];
27      }
28
```

The RemoveTweens method stops all Tween instances, deletes them, and removes them from the tweenArray.

```
29    public function RemoveTweens(Void):Void
30    {
31        for(var i in this.tweenArray)
32        {
33            this.tweenArray[i].stopEnterFrame();
34            delete this.tweenArray[i];
35        }
36
37        this.tweenArray = new Array();
38    }
39 }
```

## AS3: Singleton Pattern

Creating a class using the singleton pattern in ActionScript 3 requires a little more creativity, as private constructors are no longer allowed. The approach I use is to create a constructor that refuses instantiation and throws an error if scripts attempt to create a new TweenManager instance. As with the ActionScript 2 version of the Instance method, the code will determine if an instance property is already instantiated. If the TweenManager is already instantiated, the existing instance is used. This works because the instance property is set to an instance of the TweenManager when it is defined as a class property. Therefore, regardless of when the constructor is triggered, the class will not re-instantiate.

In order to make the TweenManager AS3-compliant, you need to import the MovieClip class since it is used to type an argument in the CreateTween function. Also, the class paths to the Tween object and the easing package have changed. The RemoveTweens function needs its return type updated to void, rather than the AS2 version of Void, with a capital V, and the stopEnterFrame method needs to be updated to stop. As in AS2, the void type is used to specify that a function cannot return a value.

These class paths have new locations in AS3.

instance is what external classes access through the Instance method.

```
1 package com.krishadlock.utils
2 {
3     import flash.display.*;
4     import fl.transitions.Tween;
5     import fl.transitions.easing.*;
6
7     public final class TweenManager
8     {
9         private static var instance:TweenManager = new
TweenManager();
```

tweenArray stores Tween instances.

Constructor functions can no longer be private. The constructor now needs to determine if an instance property exists. Since an instance property has been instantiated when it was defined as a class property above, an error is thrown if class instantiation is attempted.

instance property was instantiated when defined as a class property, so the Instance method can simply return instance.

RemoveTweens has been updated to use the Tween objects' AS3 stop method, rather than the AS2 stopEnterFrame. The return type has also been updated to void, rather than using the AS2 version, Void.

```
10    public var tweenArray:Array = new Array();
11
12    public function TweenManager()
13    {
14        if(instance)
15        {
16            throw new Error("TweenManager can only be
      accessed through TweenManager.Instance()");
17        }
18    }
19
20    public static function Instance():TweenManager
21    {
22        return instance;
23    }
24
25    public function CreateTween(mc:MovieClip, _
      property:String, _method:Function, _start:Number, _end:Number,
      _speed:Number, _type:Boolean):Tween
26        {
27            this.tweenArray.push(new Tween(mc, _property,
      _method, _start, _end, _speed, _type) );
28            return this.tweenArray[ this.tweenArray.length-1
      ];
29        }
30
31    public function RemoveTweens():void
32    {
33        for(var i in this.tweenArray)
34        {
35            this.tweenArray[i].stop();
36            delete this.tweenArray[i];
37        }
38
39        this.tweenArray = new Array();
40    }
41
42    }
43 }
```

# Scope

Scope determines how a function or property can be accessed. Scope is based on the location of a particular function or property in a code base.

## AS2: Scope

There are many issues around scoping events in ActionScript 2. The Delegate class offers a way to divert class scope dilemmas by allowing events to trigger methods, but the Delegate class also has limitations, such as not being capable of passing arguments to the function that it triggers.

```
1   import mx.utils.Delegate;
2
3   class com.yourcompanyname.view.Display extends MovieClip
4   {
5       private var _xml:XML;
6
7       public function Display(Void)
8       {
9           this._xml = new XML();
10          this._xml.ignoreWhite = true;
11          this._xml.onLoad = Delegate.create(this,
    onXMLLoaded);
12          this._xml.load("path/file.xml");
13      }
14
15      public function onXMLLoaded(Void):Void
16      {
17          trace("XML has been loaded: "+ this._xml);
18      }
19  }
```

The Delegate class diverts the XML objects' onLoad callback function to a custom method called onXMLLoaded.

Since the Delegate class had limitations, Joey Lott, coauthor of *Advanced ActionScript 3 with Design Patterns* (Adobe Press), created a class called Proxy. The Proxy class quickly made the rounds when developers realized the benefits of passing any number of arguments to a class method.

```
1   class com.yourcompanyname.utilities.Proxy
2   {
3
4       public function Proxy(Void) {}
5
```

Any arguments in addition to the two defined in the create method are added to an array and passed to the fFunction parameter.

```
6    public static function create(oTarget:Object,
     fFunction:Function):Function
7    {
8        var aParameters:Array = new Array();
9        for(var i=2; i<arguments.length; i++)
10       {
11           aParameters[i-2] = arguments[i];
12       }
13       var fProxy = function()
14       {
15           var aActualParameters =
     arguments.concat(aParameters);
16           fFunction.apply(oTarget, aActualParameters);
17       }
18       return fProxy;
19   }
20 }
```

The fFunction parameter is applied to the oTarget object, and the array of additional arguments are passed as function parameters.

The Proxy class is essentially a Delegate that allows endless arguments. Since arguments cannot be passed via the Delegate, the Proxy class helps you avoid typing numerous variables as class properties.

The create method from the Proxy class allows the _xml object as a parameter via the callback method rather than typing it as another class property.

```
1  import com.yourcompanyname.utilities.Proxy;
2
3  class com.yourcompanyname.view.Display extends MovieClip
4  {
5      public function Display(Void)
6      {
7          var _xml = new XML();
8          _xml.ignoreWhite = true;
9          _xml.onLoad = Proxy.create(this, onXMLLoaded, _xml);
10         _xml.load("path/file.xml");
11     }
12
13     public function onXMLLoaded(xml:XML):Void
14     {
15         trace("XML has been loaded: "+ this._xml);
16     }
17 }
```

Although these solutions exist, they are merely covering up inherent scope issues in AS2. Fortunately with AS3 these days are over.

## AS3: Scope

ActionScript 3 has ended the scoping nightmare: with the new event model, scoping is no longer an issue. In AS3, all events stay within the scope of the containing class. The precious Delegate class that developers had to wrap their brains around in AS2 is no longer necessary. Below is the same example from the previous section in AS3.

URLLoader and URLRequest are used to load all XML files in AS3. Loading will be covered in a later chapter. As with other packages, the path for XML has changed in AS3. The event package needs to be imported to listen for the XML objects' loading to complete.

The URLLoader is instantiated and a listener is added for the loading process of an XML file. In order to load the XML file, though, the filename must be in the form of a URLRequest.

```
1  package com.yourcompanyname.view
2  {
3      import flash.display.*;
4      import flash.net.URLLoader;
5      import flash.net.URLRequest;
6      import flash.xml.*;
7      import flash.events.*;
8
9      class Display extends MovieClip
10     {
11         public function Display()
12         {
13             var _loader:URLLoader = new URLLoader();
14         _loader.addEventListener(Event.COMPLETE, onXMLLoaded);
15         _loader.load(new URLRequest("path/file.xml"));
16         }
17
18         public function onXMLLoaded(event:Event):void
19         {
20             var loader:URLLoader =
    URLLoader(event.currentTarget);
21         var _xml:XML = new XML(loader.data);
22         trace("XML has been loaded: "+ this._xml);
23         }
24     }
25 }
```

The code is not only cleaner than versions that were possible in ActionScript 2, it just makes more sense. All objects retain scope through their events and there are no unusual hoops to jump through—it just works.

# Functions, Properties, and Keywords

WITH UNLIMITED, OPTIONAL parameters, ActionScript 3 functions provide flexibility for unexpected additions. You can also control the access to the functions you create with new attribute keywords. If you have ever used the static keyword to create a pseudoconstant in ActionScript 2, you are a resourceful developer, but you'll be happy to know that you can now create true constants.

In this chapter you'll learn the differences between function arguments and the new ...(rest) keyword, attribute keywords such as public and private, and the new protected keyword, as well as how to define constants.

# Arguments

Often confused with function parameters, arguments are actually the values of function parameters. In ActionScript 2, function parameters are defined explicitly in a function definition. There are two ways to retrieve the value of a function parameter: either through direct access to an explicit parameter variable or through the `arguments` object. In ActionScript 3, it's possible to use both these options, but a new keyword named `...(rest)` can also define the optional parameters within a function definition. The `...(rest)` keyword provides more information and offers more control over optional function parameters, and is recommended over the `arguments` object.

## AS2: Arguments

ActionScript 2 offers a number of ways to access the value of function parameters. You can access the explicit variables defined as function parameters or the values in the `arguments` object.

```
1   class ArgumentsExample
2   {
3       public function ArgumentsExample(Void)
4       {
5           this.getArgumentValues(1, 2);
6       }
7
8       private function getArgumentValues():Void
9       {
10          trace("arguments: "+ arguments.toString());
11      }
12  }
```

Optional parameters are passed to the getArgumentValues method.

When you trace the arguments object, output is arguments: 1, 2

The values within the `arguments` object are stored as an `Array`. You can access the array of values in the `arguments` object in the same order they were passed into the function, by iterating through the array or accessing the values in the `arguments` object by index. In the previous sample, 1 is the first value in the `arguments` object, and 2 is the second value in the `arguments` object. Since the `arguments` object is structured as an `Array`, determining how many parameter values were passed into a function is simple. As with any array, the `length` property determines the number of argument values and can be used to iterate the `arguments` object.

The `length` property is important because you can't simply look at how many parameters were defined in the function to determine the number of `argument` values. The `arguments` object can contain more values than the number of explicit function parameters. The following example shows how you can use the length property to iterate the values in the arguments object.

```
1   class ArgumentsExample
2   {
3       public function ArgumentsExample(Void)
4       {
5           this.getArgumentValues(1, 2);
6       }
7
8       private function getArgumentValues():Void
9       {
10          for(var i:Number=0; i<arguments.length; i++)
11          {
12              trace("argument: "+ arguments[i]);
13          }
14      }
15  }
```

When the length property is used to iterate the arguments object, the result of the trace is:
argument: 1
argument: 2

## AS3: Arguments

Although the arguments object is available in ActionScript 3, a new keyword named ...(rest) is the recommended solution for optional parameters. As with the arguments object, the ...(rest) keyword provides a way to pass any number of optional parameters to a function. One of the differences with the ...(rest) keyword is that you define it as a parameter in a function definition.

```
1   package
2   {
3       import flash.display.*;
4       public class ArgumentsExample extends Sprite
5       {
6           public function ArgumentsExample()
7           {
8               this.getRestValues(1, 2);
9           }
10
11          private function getRestValues(...rest):void
12          {
13              trace("rest: "+ rest);
14          }
15      }
16  }
```

The ...(rest) keyword is included in the function definition.

The ...(rest) keyword traces the optional parameters rest: 1, 2.

The ...(rest) keyword also lets you name the list of parameter values. Giving the parameters a name helps identify what kind of values the function is expecting and thus clarifies your code.

Tracing addNumbers would produce total: 3.

The ...(rest) parameters are given a unique name to identify the possible value types.

```
1   package
2   {
3       import flash.display.*;
4       public class ArgumentsExample extends Sprite
5       {
6           public function ArgumentsExample()
7           {
8               trace("total: "+ this.addNumbers(1, 2));
9           }
10
11          private function addNumbers(...numbers):Number
12          {
13            var total:Number = 0;
14             for(var i:uint=0; i<numbers.length; i++)
15            {
16                total += numbers[i];
17            }
18              return total;
19          }
20      }
21  }
```

The ...(rest) keyword can also be added as a function parameter after defining explicit parameters. The catch is to remember that the ...(rest) keyword can be defined only after explicit parameters because required parameters must come before optional ones. Also, the ...(rest) parameter is populated only when the number of arguments exceeds the number of explicit parameters. And unlike the arguments object, the ...(rest) keyword contains only extraneous function parameters and not explicit parameters.

true is the explicit parameter value; 1 and 2 are optional.

```
1   package
2   {
3       import flash.display.*;
4       public class ArgumentsExample extends Sprite
5       {
6           public function ArgumentsExample()
7           {
8               this.getValues(true, 1, 2);
9           }
```

```
10
11        private function getValues(explicitParam:Boolean,
   ...numbers):Void
12        {
13            trace("explicit parameter: "+ explicitParam);
14            trace("numbers: "+ numbers);
15        }
16    }
17 }
```

explicitParam is true.

numbers is 1, 2.

Although the ...(rest) keyword is similar to an Array, it is only a comma-delimited list of mixed values and does not include any of the properties or methods of an Array object, with the exception of the length property.

# Function Parameters

Function parameters are essentially the variable names of values that are passed into a function. Function parameters are fairly straightforward and have not changed in ActionScript until now.

## AS2: Function Parameters

Parameters are a fundamental part of the function definition. ActionScript 2 allows parameter typing, meaning that parameters can be specified as any native type, such as String, Boolean, Number, and so on—or can even be typed as a custom object. Typing provides control and reliability of values allowed into a function and prevents bugs by providing detailed information about your code to the Flash compiler.

```
1  class FunctionExample
2  {
3      public function FunctionExample(Void)
4      {
5          this.passArguments(1, "my string");
6      }
7
8      private function passArguments(n:Number, s:String):Void
9      {
10     }
11 }
```

passArguments can rely on n being a Number and s being a String.

## AS3: Function Parameters

Function parameters have always been a part of ActionScript. ActionScript 3 allows parameters to have default values, which essentially make them *optional* parameters. For example, if a parameter has a default value and a function call omits the parameter, the default value is used.

When default value is used, output is total: 3.5.

When default value is over-written, output is total: 4.

The round parameter is optional because it has a default value.

```
1   package
2   {
3       import flash.display.*;
4       public class FunctionExample extends Sprite
5       {
6           public function FunctionExample()
7           {
8               trace("total: "+ this.addNumbers(1, 2.5));
9               trace("total: "+ this.addNumbers(1, 2.5, true));
10          }
11
12          private function addNumbers(intOne:Number,
    intTwo:Number, round:Boolean=false):Number
13          {
14              return (round) ? Math.round(intOne + intTwo) :
    intOne + intTwo;
15          }
16      }
17  }
```

The optional parameter, named round, has a default value of false. The round parameter will remain false unless an alternate parameter value is passed in a function call. Therefore, the addNumbers sample function will not round the total it returns.

# Public Attribute Keyword

Public is the default attribute keyword for functions and properties in both ActionScript 2 and 3. Public functions and properties are completely accessible to other classes. AS3 offers a few additional features that set its public attribute apart from the AS2 version.

## AS2: Public Attribute Keyword

Public functions and properties are visible to any class in a project. The default keyword in AS2 is public, which allows any class to access class methods or properties that are not typed.

```
1   class PublicExample
2   {
3       public function PublicExample(Void)
4       {
5       }
6
7       public function ToString(Void):String
8       {
9           return "[PublicExample]";
10      }
11  }
```

ToString is public, or accessible to any class that imports Display.

Since the ToString function is public, any class that imports and instantiates the PublicExample object can access the function and retrieve the return value of ToString.

PublicExample is imported to create an instance.

Instantiate PublicExample and access the public ToString method: Object name: [PublicExample].

```
1   import PublicExample;
2   class Navigation
3   {
4       public function Navigation(Void)
5       {
6           var pExample:PublicExample = new PublicExample();
7           trace("Object name: "+ pExample.ToString());
8       }
9   }
```

## AS3: Public Attribute Keyword

In ActionScript 3, the default attribute keyword for functions and properties is also public. While attribute keywords are not required, they are standard.

The public keyword provides the same level of access to external classes as in AS2, but if a class with public functions is inherited, it's possible to override the public functions by redefining them in a subclass.

```
1   package
2   {
3       import flash.display.*;
```

```
 4      public class PublicExample extends Sprite
 5      {
 6          public function PublicExample()
 7          {
 8          }
 9
10          public function ToString():String
11          {
12              return "[PublicExample]";
13          }
14      }
15  }
```

ToString returns a string representation of the class.

Subclasses can return new values and invoke code differently within methods that they override, but must accept and return the same value types. For example, if a superclass contains a method that returns a String, a subclass that overrides the method cannot return a Boolean. Instead, the return type must be a String.

```
 1  package
 2  {
 3      public class Navigation extends PublicExample
 4      {
 5          public function Navigation()
 6          {
 7              super();
 8          }
 9
10          public override function ToString():String
11          {
12              return "[Navigation]";
13          }
14      }
15  }
```

PublicExample is the superclass.

ToString must return a String since the overwritten method returns a String.

If you wanted to return the hierarchy of classes when calling the ToString function, you could also invoke the superclass version of the ToString function.

```
 1  package
 2  {
 3      public class Navigation extends PublicExample
 4      {
```

PublicExample is the superclass.

```
5    public function Navigation()
6    {
7        super();
8        trace("Object name: "+ this.ToString());
9    }
10
11    public override function ToString():String
12    {
13        return super.ToString() + "[Navigation]";
14    }
15  }
16 }
```

The output of the trace is Object name: [PublicExample] [Navigation].

# Private Attribute Keyword

As more attribute keywords have been added to the ActionScript language, some of the existing functionality has changed to accommodate the additions. The private attribute keyword is a prime example: At first glance the changes may seem minor, but they actually require the addition of an entirely new attribute keyword.

## AS2: Private Attribute Keyword

In ActionScript 2 the private attribute keyword is used to restrict access to methods and properties. Where public allows access to any class, private limits access to the class that defines it and any subclasses of the defining class.

```
1  class PrivateExample
2  {
3      public function PrivateExample(Void)
4      {
5      }
6
7      private function render(Void):Void
8      {
9      }
10 }
```

Only the defining class or subclasses can invoke code within the render function.

The private keyword is extremely useful when writing methods or properties that are either of no use to other classes or contain information that needs to be kept secure.

# AS3: Private Attribute Keyword

In ActionScript 3 the private attribute keyword is a lot more private than in AS2. Not only is a private function, property, or namespace inaccessible from other classes, private items can no longer be inherited either. If you need to keep a function, property, or namespace hidden from other classes, but you still want them to be inherited, you can use a new keyword called protected. The protected keyword allows access only to subclasses. Even classes in the same package are not allowed access through protected.

```
 1  package
 2  {
 3      import flash.display.*;
 4      public class PrivateExample extends Sprite
 5      {
 6          public function PrivateExample()
 7          {
 8              this.initialize();
 9          }
10
11          private function initialize():void
12          {
13          }
14
15          protected function render():void
16          {
17          }
18      }
19  }
```

Only the defining class can invoke the initialize method; even subclasses cannot reach private methods.

The initialize method can be invoked only by the defining class or any of its subclasses.

Since the protected keyword allows access to subclasses, subclasses can define new values for the protected properties that they inherit. Subclasses cannot override protected functions, however.

```
 1  package
 2  {
 3      public class Navigation extends PrivateExample
 4      {
 5          public function Navigation()
 6          {
 7              super.render();
 8          }
 9      }
10  }
```

PrivateExample is the superclass.

render can be used by this subclass because it is protected, but render cannot be overridden.

# Defining Constants

Many ActionScript developers have been resourceful in finding ways to create workarounds and build functionality that wasn't intended by the language's creators. For example, we've all created custom constants to store important data for use throughout an application. But custom constants are no longer necessary in ActionScript. At last, the `const` keyword lets you define a property that cannot be altered, remaining the same in all situations.

## AS2: Defining Constants

In ActionScript 2 there was no true way to define constants. Developers would often resort to creating `static` variables as constants that they could add to a class in order to keep them easily accessible.

```
1   class Status
2   {
3       static public var PASSED:Number = 1;
4       static public var COMPLETE:Number = 2;
5       static public var FAILED:Number = 3;
6       static public var INCOMPLETE:Number = 4;
7   }
```

Allowing an external class to change the values of your constants can lead to bugs that are very hard to find. Plus, it's completely insecure: a knowledgeable user with malicious intentions could change the constants and break your code.

## AS3: Defining Constants

In ActionScript 3 you no longer have to write custom code for constants, as in AS2. Now you can use the `const` keyword to define a property as a constant, so that in all situations the value remains the same and is reliable.

The Status class can be used anywhere, and the values of the constants always remain the same.

```
1    package
2    {
3        public class Status
4        {
5            static public const PASSED:Number = 1;
6            static public const COMPLETE:Number = 2;
7            static public const FAILED:Number = 3;
8            static public const INCOMPLETE:Number = 4;
9        }
10   }
```

CHAPTER 5

# Scope

ATTEMPTING TO CORRECTLY target objects in Flash often creates ActionScript bugs for new Flash developers. Flash's reliance on movie timelines can make it hard to understand *scope*, or where variables can be referenced within the code. But it's not just the timeline—the inner workings of a SWF file are unlike any other language. Scope issues in Flash can be confusing because of the complex arrangement of the timeline, movie clips, movie clips embedded in movie clips, buttons, buttons embedded in movie clips, and so on.

Luckily, the introduction of the display list and class-based architecture in ActionScript 3 eliminate most of the scope issues that were a problem in ActionScript 2. And as covered in Chapter 3, packages and classes help organize your code, thus making the scope of your objects easier to grasp.

In this chapter, you will learn how scope is handled in AS3.

# Root

Scope can get awfully tricky in Flash, but when all else fails, developers have always been able to target _root. This property is always accessible and always at the level of the timeline in the current Flash movie. But what is _root now that the display list exists, and how do you target it? You definitely don't want to skip this section because the _root you've come to know is very different in AS3.

## AS2: Root

You shouldn't have to tie a class to the root of a Flash movie if you have a solid class-based structure. Doing so actually defeats the purpose of writing reusable code!

That said, although it's not a best practice and is even considered a hack, it is still possible to make calls to _root in ActionScript 2.

```
1   class RootExample
2   {
3       public function RootExample(Void)
4       {
5           trace("root: "+ _root);
6       }
7   }
```

The output of the trace is root: _level0.

In AS2, _root refers to the main timeline, which is _level0. The problem is that the main timeline can change when you start creating more complex applications, combining movies, and loading one movie into another.

Issues arise because loaded movies with references to the _root call the _root of the SWF that loaded them, rather than the _root of their own SWF. You can avoid this problem by using the MovieClip object's _lockroot property. Simply set the _lockroot property to true on the main timeline of the loaded MovieClip; this ensures that any calls to _root in the loaded SWF will point to the loaded SWF's _root. Still, while technically possible, this functionality is a bit confusing and easy to make a mess of.

# AS3: Root

**NOTE** Like many other properties in ActionScript 3, root has dropped the underscore, making it root rather than _root.

The organization of objects has changed dramatically in ActionScript 3; root still exists, but not as a reference to the main timeline. The root property is now based on the tree structure of the object that is targeting its root property. The top DisplayObject in the current display list's tree structure is now the root.

All DisplayObjects now have a root property, but root does not always refer to the same object. It may seem confusing, but it actually makes a lot of sense. For example, if you were to declare a document class, name it RootExample, and trace the root property from the constructor, you would get a reference to the Stage object.

**NOTE** There is no more need for the _lockroot property, as it is essentially always in effect.

```
1   package
2   {
3       import flash.display.*;
4       public class RootExample extends Sprite
5       {
6           public function RootExample()
7           {
8               super();
9               trace("root: "+ this.root);
10          }
11      }
12  }
```

The output of the trace is root: [object Stage].

In this case the root DisplayObject of our custom RootExample class is the Stage. The document class is the Stage, which also happens to be the top-most DisplayObject in the current tree structure.

If you add children to the DisplayObject, the tree structure changes, making the DisplayObject the root of its own tree structure and the root of its children.

```
1   package
2   {
3       import flash.display.*;
4       public class RootExample extends Sprite
5       {
6           public function RootExample()
7           {
8               trace("root: "+ this.root);
9               this.addNavigation();
10          }
```

The output of the trace is root: [object Display].

```
11
12          private function addNavigation():void
13          {
14              var nav:Navigation = Navigation(this.addChild(
    new Navigation()));
15              trace("nav root: "+ nav.root);
16          }
17      }
18  }
```

Instantiate and add a Navigation object to the stage.

The output of the trace is nav root: [object Display].

The root of the Navigation instance is the RootExample class because the RootExample class is the top object in the structure. However, until the navigation instance is added to the display list, the root value of Navigation is null. Therefore a trace of the root property from the constructor function in the Navigation class will trace null, but after the navigation has been added, the trace will contain the root of the object.

```
1  package
2  {
3      import flash.display.*;
4      public class Navigation extends Sprite
5      {
6          public function Navigation()
7          {
8              trace("root: "+ this.root);
9          }
10      }
11  }
```

The output of the trace is root: [object null].

# Stage

All visible objects reside on the stage. Timeline-based animations are created on the stage; and buttons, movie clips, graphics and components are added to the stage. In ActionScript 3, the stage hasn't changed, but the way it is accessed is new.

## AS2: Stage

In ActionScript 2, Stage is a globally accessible class. This means that from any object and class, anywhere in your Flash movie, you can call Stage and it will be available.

Stage is a pretty basic class, with only six static properties and two event handlers, but you can use it to determine the stage size, set a movie to full screen, set a movie's scale mode, or turn the Flash player context menu on and off.

```
1   class StageExample
2   {
3       public function StageExample(Void)
4       {
5           Stage.showMenu = false;
6           Stage.scaleMode = 'noScale';
7       }
8   }
```

The context menu will not contain default options, and the stage will not scale if the movie is scaled.

## AS3: Stage

In ActionScript 3, stage is the root of the display list and the property with the nearest value to the _root property in ActionScript 2. The stage property refers to the same Stage object, regardless of the targeting object. Flash has only one Stage object, and all objects added to the display list have that stage property in common.

The Stage object is a little more robust than it used to be, with additional classes for alignment, quality, scale mode, and display state constants. The Stage class now includes 16 properties, not counting the inherited properties. Although the Stage class is no longer globally accessible, it is still easily accessed through the stage property of a DisplayObject instance. For example, if you created a document class named StageExample, you could access the Stage object via the inherited stage property.

```
1    package
2    {
3        import flash.display.*;
4        public class StageExample extends Sprite
5        {
6            public function StageExample()
7            {
8                trace("stage: "+ this.stage);
9            }
10       }
11   }
```

The output of this trace is stage: [object Stage].

Our StageExample class inherits the stage property because it extends the Sprite class, which ultimately extends the DisplayObject. With access to the stage property, you can access all the properties that the Stage object offers. In order to achieve the same results as you did in the AS2 example, you would access the inherited `stage` property.

```
 1   package
 2   {
 3       import flash.display.*;
 4       public class StageExample extends Sprite
 5       {
 6           public function StageExample()
 7           {
 8               this.stage.showDefaultContextMenu = false;
 9               this.stage.scaleMode = StageScaleMode.NO_SCALE;
10           }
11       }
12   }
```

> With a value of false, the context menu will not contain the defaults.

> The `stage` is not scalable when set to `NO_SCALE`.

You'll notice a few differences in the AS3 version of this code.

First of all, the `stage` has a new property called `showDefaultContextMenu`. This property is still a Boolean with the same functionality, which sets the display mode of the default context menu items to visible or not visible.

The `scaleMode` is a bit different, as well. Rather than using a literal string to set the value, you can now rely on the `StageScaleMode` class, accessible through the `flash.display` package that you are already importing to inherit `Sprite`. The `StageScaleMode` class has constants that represent the string values available in AS2, thus eliminating the need to rely on your own typing skills to input the values and triggering the autocomplete feature in the Actions panel. In addition to the `StageScaleMode`, the `Stage` object also offers classes that provide values for alignment, quality, and display state.

# Parent

Targeting the parent object is a good way to traverse a tree structure within a Flash movie. *Parent* always refers to the object that contains the current object. While the concept of parent has essentially stayed the same between ActionScript 2 and ActionScript 3, the way you access it has changed.

## AS2: Parent

In ActionScript 2, `_parent` is a global property that can be used to refer to the objects that are a level above the current object, often referred to as *parent objects*. The parent chain essentially traverses up the container hierarchy to `_level0` because all visual objects start at the `_level0`, or main timeline.

**Figure 5.1** *An example of object structure on the main timeline in Flash.*

In **Figure 5.1**, the parent object of `_level0.instance1.instance2` is `_level0.instance1`, and the parent object of `_level0.instance1` is `_level0`, or the main timeline. To access the parent object of each movie clip instance, you simply target the `_parent` property. Adding the following code on the timeline of the middle square would produce a reference to the parent.

The output of the `trace` is parent of `middle square: _level0.instance1`.

```
1    trace("parent of middle square: "+ this._parent);
```

Accessing the `_parent` property is useful in situations where you may not know the name of the parent object. Not knowing the name of the parent object is common, as the parent object may change based on externally loaded Flash movies.

## AS3: Parent

A `parent` property still exists in ActionScript 3, but it is accessed differently than in previous versions of ActionScript.

**NOTE** Like many other properties in ActionScript 3, parent has dropped the underscore before the name, making the property parent rather than _parent.

The difference in how the `parent` property is accessed is due to the new display-list structure of Flash movies. Like the `stage` and `root` properties, the `parent` property is accessible only from a `DisplayObject` that is actively part of the display list.

**Figure 5.2** *An example of object structure on the main timeline in Flash.*

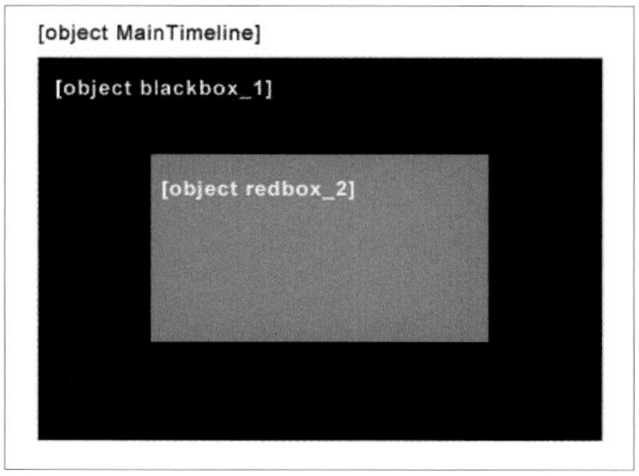

In **Figure 5.2** you have the same structure as in Figure 5.1, but the differences are quite clear. There are no longer references to _level0 or to numbered instance names; rather, there are references to the actual objects based on their library names and where they reside in the display list. If you were to add the following ActionScript to the middle square, you would get a reference to the parent as the value.

The output of the trace is parent of middle square: [object blackbox_1].

```
1  trace("parent of middle square: "+ this.parent);
```

# Function and Method Definitions

Along with the class-scope updates that were mentioned in the Scope section of Chapter 3, function and method definitions have been improved in a number of ways in ActionScript 3. A primary example of how the display list has had a positive effect on the scope of function and method definitions is the removal of the Delegate. In this section you'll learn about some additional changes in AS3 and how the new display structure improves the entire ActionScript language.

## AS2: Function and Method Definitions

ActionScript 2 makes it easy to call public methods in other classes, pass parameters, and even receive a response. In the following example, the code will render a Web site in Flash. A class called Navigation will be imported and will contain page names that are used in a Web site.

pages will be used to store an array of page names.

```
1  class Navigation
2  {
3      public var pages:Array;
4      public function Navigation(Void)
5      {
6          this.pages = new Array("Home", "About us");
7      }
8
9      public function GetPageCount(Void):Number
10     {
11         return this.pages.length;
12     }
13 }
```

Before you do anything with the navigation pages, it may be important to retrieve a count of items in the array to determine how you will render the list.

```
1  import Navigation;
2  class DefinitionExample
3  {
4      public function DefinitionExample(Void)
5      {
6          var nav:Navigation = new Navigation();
7          trace(nav.GetPageCount());
8      }
9  }
```

GetPageCount is a public method in the Navigation class.

This is a typical class interaction: instantiating a class, calling a public method, and receiving a response based on the return type. The functionality gets more complicated as soon as you want to return a method from the Navigation class that references the pages array. The following code starts by making the getPageCount function private and creating a new public method called GetPages. The GetPages method takes a String parameter, which defines what function to return: this way you can easily add more private methods to the class and return them based on the parameter.

```
 1  class Navigation
 2  {
 3      public var pages:Array;
 4      public function Navigation(Void)
 5      {
 6          this.pages = new Array("Home", "About us");
 7      }
 8
 9      private function getPageCount(Void):Number
10      {
11          trace(this);
12          return this.pages.length;
13      }
14
15      public function GetPages(option:String):Function
16      {
17          switch(option)
18          {
19              case "count":
20                  return this.getPageCount;
21                  break;
22              default:
23                  return null;
24          }
```

GetPages takes a String parameters value and determines what class method to return.

```
25          }
26  }
```

The previous example makes sense in theory and is an easy way to organize some functions into one public method call, but if you try to access the
returned function, you'll get a response of undefined.

```
1   import Navigation;
2   class DefinitionExample
3   {
4       public function DefinitionExample(Void)
5       {
6           var nav:Navigation = new Navigation();
7           trace(this);
8           var pageCount:Function = nav.GetPages("count");
9           trace(pageCount());
10      }
11  }
```

The trace of this is
[object Object].

The trace of pageCount is
undefined.

Unfortunately, the scope of the this keyword is not retained. You will get a
valid response from GetPages, but the trace of the this keyword will return
undefined, and obviously this.pages will be undefined as well. The good
news is that the code works in AS3.

## AS3: Function and Method Definitions

With bound methods or method closures in ActionScript 3, returning functions don't have the same limitations as in ActionScript 2. Let's take the
example from the previous section and make the necessary updates for
AS3 compatibility. First, we'll update the Navigation class.

The Navigation class
needs to be wrapped in
a package.

```
1   package
2   {
3       import flash.display.*;
4       public class Navigation extends Sprite
5       {
6           private var pages:Array;
7           public function Navigation()
8           {
9               this.pages = new Array("Home", "About us");
10          }
11
12          private function getPageCount():Number
13          {
```

```
14            trace(this);
15            return this.pages.length;
16        }
17
18        public function GetPages(option:String):Function
19        {
20            switch(option)
21            {
22                case "count":
23                    return this.getPageCount;
24                    break;
25                default:
26                    return null;
27            }
28        }
29    }
30 }
```

To run the code, you now need to make the necessary updates to the DefinitionExample class and link the DefinitionExample class to the Flash movie as the document class.

Import Navigation for later instantiation.

The Sprite class is inherited since the timeline is not being used.

The trace of this is [object Display].

The trace of pageCount is 2.

```
1  package
2  {
3      import flash.display.*;
4      import Navigation;
5      public class DefinitionExample extends Sprite
6      {
7          public function DefinitionExample()
8          {
9              super();
10             var nav:Navigation = new Navigation();
11             trace(this);
12             var pageCount:Function = nav.GetPages("count");
13             trace(pageCount());
14         }
15     }
16 }
```

Because AS3 keeps the this keyword bound to the parent class of the function, the scope of the this keyword is not lost and the functionality now works. This means that functions returned from classes with references to this will now refer to the class that defined the method and scope will not be lost, which resulted in an undefined return value in AS2.

CHAPTER 6

# Timing

CREATING YOUR OWN timer is common in Flash movies and is especially important when you do not want to rely on the timeline. Playback controls, countdown clocks, or any other form of time measurement are examples of timing functionality.

In this chapter, we'll compare the timing options in ActionScript 2 and 3, and look at two new AS3 classes, called `Timer` and `TimerEvent`, that handle timer events.

# Setting a Time Interval

Developers use time intervals in Flash projects to repetitively call a function or class method. Both versions of ActionScript let you use the setInterval function to create this functionality; however, AS3 offers a more robust solution using the Timer and TimerEvent classes.

## AS2: Setting a Time Interval

The most efficient way to set a time interval in ActionScript 2 is using the setInterval function. setInterval is a global function (so it is accessible without the need to import a class) that can repetitively call a function or class method at a predefined time interval.

I was once part of an e-learning project (for an airline) that heavily relied on the setInterval function. Students were required to view each screen for a specific amount of time in order for the client to meet certain federal regulations. Unfortunately, setInterval was the only way to accomplish this in Flash, and it is not the most reliable function.

The setInterval function is unreliable because the results are based on the frame rate and available memory of the Flash movie, as well as the defined interval. Luckily, the e-learning course was low-bandwidth, so the frame rate and delay were the only variables that needed to be adjusted to create an accurate time interval. Intervals run in milliseconds; therefore, adjusting the interval based on the frame rate is important. For example, a Flash movie that runs at 10 frames per second (fps) runs in 100-millisecond intervals. If the frame rate and interval are not in sync, the interval is called as close as possible and therefore is not always accurate.

The following code is a simple example of how you could use the setInterval function to reliably call a class method that loads a new screen every five seconds in a Flash movie that has a frame rate of 10 fps.

A Flash movie running 10 fps with a 5000-millisecond interval should execute every five seconds.

```
1   class TimerExample
2   {
3       public function TimerExample(Void)
4       {
5           setInterval(this, "loadScreen", 5000);
6       }
7
8       private function loadScreen(Void):Void
9       {
10          trace("Code to load a screen goes here");
```

```
11          }
12      }
```

# AS3: Setting a Time Interval

In ActionScript3, you can set a time interval via the `setInterval` function or the `Timer` and `TimerEvent` classes. To accomplish the same functionality as in the previous AS2 example with the `setInterval` function, the call must be slightly modified.

In AS3, `setInterval` requires the `flash.utils` package to be imported, yet only calls for two arguments. The first argument is the class method that the interval will execute; but rather than defining the class method as a string, the `setInterval` function takes the literal function name. The second parameter in the `setInterval` call is the execution time in milliseconds.

```
1   package
2   {
3       import flash.utils.*;
4
5       public class TimerExample
6       {
7           public function TimerExample()
8           {
9               setInterval(loadScreen, 5000);
10          }
11
12          private function loadScreen():void
13          {
14              trace("Code to load a screen goes here");
15          }
16      }
17  }
```

flash.utils is imported for setInterval. *(pointing to line 3)*

loadScreen is literal, rather than a string. *(pointing to line 9)*

As mentioned earlier, AS3 also offers a more robust solution to set a time interval, via the `Timer` and `TimerEvent` classes. The `Timer` class can be imported into your scripts to use properties and methods providing functionality that had to be custom written in previous versions of ActionScript. The `TimerEvent` class works in unison with the `Timer` as the event handler for time-based events.

Although the `Timer` class is more robust than the `setInterval` function, they both have timing issues with the frame rate and available memory of Flash movies. The following example uses the `Timer` and `TimerEvent` classes to create the same time interval as in the previous example. The solution is streamlined and more reliable because custom code is not necessary.

Timer and TimerEvent are imported to create a time interval.

Timer is instantiated with a 5000-millisecond interval, and a TimerEvent is added.

start initiates the interval.

```
1   package
2   {
3       import flash.utils.Timer;
4       import flash.events.TimerEvent;
5
6       public class TimerExample
7       {
8           public function TimerExample()
9           {
10              var myTimer = new Timer(5000);
11              myTimer.addEventListener(TimerEvent.TIMER,
    loadScreen);
12              myTimer.start();
13          }
14
15          private function loadScreen(e:TimerEvent):void
16          {
17              trace("Code to load a screen goes here");
18          }
19      }
20  }
```

# Keeping Count

One of the most common uses of a timer is to keep count. Keeping count is necessary for purposes such as determining when to display an item on the stage, tracking the time a user has interacted with a particular item, or even restricting users from specific interactions for a certain amount of time. Keeping count in ActionScript 3 is a bit different than it is in ActionScript 2 if you use the Timer and TimerEvent classes.

## AS2: Keeping Count

As with all timing functionality in ActionScript 2, custom code must be written to handle each situation. In order to keep track of the time an interval has run, the timing must be accurate and a class property must exist.

As mentioned earlier, accurate timing is a balance of the time interval, frame rate (fps), and available Flash movie memory. The class property needed to keep count is used to store the number of times the interval has run. The class property can then be used in calculations to determine the amount of time that has passed since an interval began. In the following example, a class property named count has been added to the TimerExample class.

```
1   class TimerExample
2   {
3       private var count:Number;
4
5       public function TimerExample(Void)
6       {
7           this.count = 5;
8           setInterval(this, "countdown", 1000);
9       }
10
11      private function loadScreen(Void):Void
12      {
13          trace("Code to load a screen goes here");
14      }
15
16      private function countdown(Void):Void
17      {
18          if(this.count == 0)
19          {
20          this.count = 5;
21          this.loadScreen();
22          }
23          this.count--;
24          trace("Time left: "+ String(this.count));
25      }
26  }
```

A Flash movie running at 10 fps with a 1000-millisecond interval should execute every second.

The countdown method decrements the count property and executes loadScreen if the count is 0.

## AS3: Keeping Count

Keeping count in ActionScript 3 is extremely easy because the Timer class contains a property that keeps track of the interval count for you. The Timer class offers a handy property named currentCount, which contains the total number of times the Timer has fired since starting.

In the following example, the currentCount property is used in place of the custom count property from AS2.

Timer and TimerEvent are imported to create a time interval.

Timer is set to an interval of 1000 milliseconds to run the countdown method every second.

start eliminates the need to re-instantiate the Timer.

currentCount eliminates the need to create a class property to keep count.

```
1  package
2  {
3      import flash.utils.Timer;
4      import flash.events.TimerEvent;
5
6      public class TimerExample
7      {
8          private var myTimer:Timer;
9
10         public function TimerExample()
11         {
12             this.myTimer = new Timer(1000);
13             this.myTimer.addEventListener(TimerEvent.TIMER,
   countdown);
14             this.myTimer.start();
15         }
16
17         private function loadScreen():void
18         {
19             trace("Code to load a screen goes here");
20             this.myTimer.start();
21         }
22
23         private function countdown(e:TimerEvent):void
24         {
25             var count:Number = (5-this.myTimer.currentCount);
26             trace("Time left: "+ String(count));
27             if(count == 0)
28             {
29                 this.myTimer.reset();
30                 this.loadScreen();
31             }
32         }
33
34     }
35 }
```

# Delaying Code

If you simply want to delay the execution of code in a project, you can use the setTimeout function in either version of ActionScript. AS3 also offers a way to achieve the same functionality with additional options via the Timer and TimerEvent classes.

## AS2: Delaying Code

ActionScript 2 offers setTimeout as a global function. Using setTimeout is similar to using the setInterval function. The difference is that an interval is recurring, while a timeout executes only once. setTimeout is used as a way to delay a function or class method, rather than to create recurring functionality.

A Flash movie running 10 fps with a 5000-millisecond timeout should execute the callback function with a five-second delay.

```
1  class TimerExample
2  {
3      public function TimerExample(Void)
4      {
5          setTimeout(loadScreen, 5000);
6      }
7
8      private function loadScreen(Void):Void
9      {
10         trace("Code to load a screen goes here");
11     }
12 }
```

## AS3: Delaying Code

The exact same functionality as in the previous example can be produced with the setTimeout function in ActionScript 3 if the flash.utils package is imported.

flash.utils is imported to use the setTimeout function.

```
1  package
2  {
3      import flash.utils.*;
4
5      public class TimerExample
6      {
7          public function TimerExample()
8          {
```

A Flash movie running 10 fps with a 5000-millisecond timeout should execute the callback function with a five-second delay.

```
 9            setTimeout(loadScreen, 5000);
10        }
11
12        private function loadScreen():void
13        {
14            trace("Code to load a screen goes here");
15        }
16    }
17 }
```

AS3 offers the same functionality with the Timer class. The Timer class allows the option of one additional parameter that determines how many times a Timer executes. For instance, you can recreate the same functionality as in the setTimeout function by adding 1 as the third parameter (called repeatCount), or you can add any other number you choose. The following example shows the same functionality as in the previous setTimeout function.

Timer and TimerEvent are imported to create the same functionality as in setTimeout.

A Flash movie running 10 fps with a 5000-millisecond Timer and a repeatCount of 1 should execute with a five-second delay.

start eliminates the need to re-instantiate the Timer.

```
 1 package
 2 {
 3     import flash.utils.Timer;
 4     import flash.events.TimerEvent;
 5
 6     public class TimerExample
 7     {
 8         public function TimerExample()
 9         {
10             var myTimer = new Timer(5000, 1);
11             myTimer.addEventListener(TimerEvent.TIMER,
loadScreen);
12             myTimer.start();
13         }
14
15         private function loadScreen(e:TimerEvent):void
16         {
17             trace("Code to load a screen goes here");
18         }
19     }
20 }
```

CHAPTER 7

# Text

ONE OF THE most valuable design features in Flash is the ability to embed any font in a SWF file and have it render the same on any platform. Flash also lets you display dynamic text as an embedded font, embed and format fonts dynamically, and apply text-field listeners to trigger events based on specific user interactions.

In this chapter you will learn how to embed fonts, dynamically create and format text fields, and replace ActionScript 2 text-field callback-function properties with the new text events available in ActionScript 3.

# Font Usage

With the embed feature, Flash lets you use any font from your computer on the Web. When a font is embedded, end users do not need to have the font on their system to see the result. The extent of what can be done with embedded fonts is limited by the version of ActionScript you are using: AS3 introduces some additions to the functionality that help make the switch from AS2 to AS3 impossible to pass up.

## AS2: Font Usage

Embedding fonts in ActionScript 2 is incredibly beneficial, allowing dynamic copy to be displayed in any font in a Flash movie. This functionality lets you develop applications that can import dynamic data while still maintaining the integrity of a design.

To embed a font in a text field and dynamically render text with ActionScript, you first need to create a dynamic text field on the stage. Once you have created the text field, you must provide an instance name in the Properties panel to allow access to the field in your code. To embed a specific font in the text field, choose a font from the Properties panel and choose the embed button. **Figure 7.1** shows an example of how to embed a font in a dynamic text field.

**Figure 7.1** *Fonts can be embedded in a dynamic text field.*

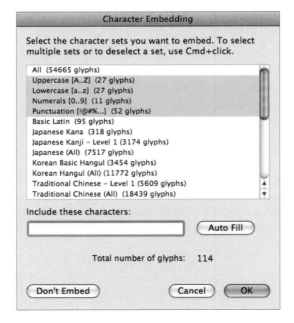

With the embedded font, you can now add text through ActionScript and maintain the integrity of the font used in your design. Here's an example:

The text field created in the Flash movie is defined in the class.

Text can be applied to the text field, and the font will continue to render.

```
1   class TextFieldExample extends MovieClip
2   {
3       private var txtField:TextField;
4
5       public function TextFieldExample()
6       {
7           this.txtField.text = "Dynamic text";
8       }
9
10  }
```

## AS3: Font Usage

To achieve the same functionality in ActionScript 3 as in the AS2 example, you would use almost the exact same code. The only differences are that you need to wrap your class in a package, and you do not need to declare your text field as a class property.

```
1   package
2   {
3       import flash.display.*;
4
5       public class TextFieldExample extends Sprite
6       {
7           public function TextFieldExample()
8           {
9               this.txtField.text = "Dynamic text";
10          }
11      }
12  }
```

AS3 also has a new class named Font. The Font class has been added to manage embedded fonts in SWF files. The Font class cannot be instantiated through ActionScript, but when a font is embedded in your Flash movie, the properties and methods of the Font class can be accessed for the embedded font. The properties include fontName, fontStyle, and fontType; and the methods include enumerateFonts, hasGlyphs, and registerFont.

The functionality the Font class offers is pretty amazing. For example, you can use the enumerateFonts method to retrieve an array of the available embedded fonts in a Flash movie. You could then use the array of fonts to list the available fonts in a movie. With a bit of customization, you can use enumerateFonts to let users choose fonts in a Flash movie.

The following example uses the enumerateFonts method to retrieve an array of the available fonts to the Flash movie. The array is then iterated to trace each font name, type (embedded or device), and style (regular, bold, italic, and so on).

```
1   package
2   {
3       import flash.display.*;
4       import flash.text.Font;
5
6       public class TextFieldExample extends Sprite
7       {
8           public function TextFieldExample()
9           {
10              var allFonts:Array = Font.enumerateFonts(true);
11              for(var i:int=0; i<allFonts.length; i++)
12              {
13                  trace("Font name: "+ allFonts[i].fontName,
                            "\nFont type: "+ allFonts[i].fontType,
                            "\nFont style: "+ allFonts[i].fontStyle,
                            "\n--------");
14              }
15          }
16      }
17  }
```

enumerateFonts retrieves all the fonts used in the Flash movie.

allFonts is iterated to retrieve all the fonts' names, types, and styles.

# TextField

The ability to create dynamic text fields with ActionScript has made Flash a viable option for dynamic application development. Flash can receive external data, create a dynamic text field, and display the external data based on user interaction. In this section, you will see the differences in how dynamic text fields are created in AS2 and AS3.

## AS2: TextField

Creating a dynamic text field in ActionScript 2 is fairly straightforward. The MovieClip class has a method named createTextField, which lets you create text fields dynamically. Below is an example of how a

TextField is dynamically created with AS2 and added to a Flash movie via the createTextField method. Notice that the MovieClip class must be extended in order to use the createTextField method.

createTextField is inherited from the MovieClip class.

The dynamically created text field is a TextField class instance.

```
1   class TextFieldExample extends MovieClip
2   {
3       public function TextFieldExample()
4       {
5           var txtField:TextField = this.createTextField(
    "txtField",1,100,100,100,100);
6           txtField.multiline = true;
7           txtField.wordWrap = true;
8           txtField.border = true;
9           txtField.text = "Dynamic text";
10      }
11
12  }
```

## AS3: TextField

The architectural changes in ActionScript 3 allow direct instantiation of the TextField class through the TextField constructor, eliminating the need to use the MovieClip class for dynamic text field creation.

The following example shows how the TextField class can be instantiated and added to the display list via the addChild method.

Import the TextField and TextFieldAutoSize classes to instantiate and format a text field.

Create a class property to provide access throughout the class.

```
1   package
2   {
3       import flash.display.*;
4       import flash.text.TextField;
5       import flash.text.TextFieldAutoSize;
6
7       public class TextFieldExample extends Sprite
8       {
9           private var label:TextField;
10          public function TextFieldExample()
11          {
12              this.createTextField();
13              this.setLabel();
14          }
15
```

```
16    private function setLabel():void
17    {
18        this.label.text = "Dynamic embedded font";
19    }
20
21    private function createTextField():void
22    {
23        this.label = new TextField();
24        this.label.autoSize = TextFieldAutoSize.LEFT;
25        this.label.background = true;
26        this.label.border = true;
27        addChild(this.label);
28    }
29   }
30 }
```

Direct instantiation of the `TextField` class eliminates the need for the `MovieClip` class.

The `TextFieldAutoSize` class is used instead of simple strings.

`addChild` is inherited from the `DisplayObjectContainer` by the `Sprite` class.

# Text Events

Text-based events exist in both versions of ActionScript, but are now completely integrated into the ActionScript 3 architecture. The integration of events into AS3 has eliminated the need for callback-function properties and has made all events, including text events, function in the same universal way.

## AS2: Text Events

In ActionScript 2, `TextField` events are handled by callback-function properties. Unfortunately, when you use callback-function properties, you also have to use the `Delegate` class and you lose the arguments that are passed to the callback functions. Your script may get quite complicated because of the additional class properties you must create in order to access the arguments in the callback function.

In the following example, an event-listener object is added to a dynamically created text field. The event listener fires the `TextField` object's `onChanged` callback-function property when a user types in the text field.

```
1  import mx.utils.Delegate;
2
3  class TextFieldExample extends MovieClip
4  {
```

```
5      public function TextFieldExample()
6      {
7          var txtField:TextField = this.createTextField(
       "txtField",1,100,100,100,100);
8          txtField.multiline = true;
9          txtField.wordWrap = true;
10         txtField.border = true;
11         txtField.type = "input";
12
13         var txtListener:Object = new Object();
14         txtListener.onChanged = Delegate.create(this,
       onTextFieldChanged);
15         txtField.addListener(txtListener);
16     }
17
18     private function onTextFieldChanged(Void):Void
19     {
20         trace("onTextFieldChanged");
21     }
22
23 }
```

txtField is set to input text, so users can enter text.

A listener object is added to dispatch events when a user enters text in the text field.

onTextFieldChanged is triggered when text is entered in the text field.

## AS3: Text Events

In addition to the inherent TextField class events, ActionScript 3 offers a TextEvent class that handles hyperlinks and text-field input. This new solution to handling events is much more robust than AS2's callback-function properties, as events can be scoped, extended, and implemented without adding a lot of custom code.

The following example uses the TextFieldType class to set a text field as input text and the TextEvent class to listen and fire events based on user input.

```
1  package
2  {
3      import flash.display.*;
4      import flash.text.TextField;
5      import flash.text.TextFieldType;
6      import flash.events.TextEvent;
7
8      public class TextFieldExample extends Sprite
9      {
```

TextFieldType is imported to set a text field to input text.

Import TextEvent to listen for and fire events based on user input.

```
10        private var label:TextField;
11
12        public function TextFieldExample()
13        {
14            this.createTextField();
15            this.label.addEventListener(TextEvent.TEXT_INPUT,
     this.onTextFieldChanged);
16        }
17
18        private function createTextField():void
19        {
20            this.label = new TextField();
21            this.label.width = 200;
22            this.label.height = 50;
23            this.label.background = true;
24            this.label.border = true;
25            this.label.type = TextFieldType.INPUT;
26            addChild(this.label);
27        }
28
29        private function onTextFieldChanged(event:TextEvent):
     void
30        {
31            trace("onTextFieldChanged: "+ event);
32        }
33    }
34 }
```

TextEvent.TEXT_INPUT is used to fire an event when a user enters text in the text field.

The text-field type is set to input. Users can enter text in an input text field.

onTextFieldChanged is fired when text is entered in the text field. onTextFieldChanged is passed a TextEvent object, which contains information about the event.

# Formatting

Text formatting is essentially the same in both versions of ActionScript, with the exception of a few new properties in AS3. But the new text-formatting properties are integrated into the new display architecture of AS3 and are therefore important to understand.

In this section, you will learn how to create a TextFormat object and apply it to text fields in AS2 and AS3.

## AS2: Formatting

Text formatting is pretty simple to set up once you know how you would like your text to display. When applying a text format to a text field, you first need to dynamically create a text field with ActionScript. Once you create the text field, you can create a TextFormat instance, set formatting properties, and, finally, apply the formatting to a text field.

The following example shows how easily a text field can be dynamically created with ActionScript and formatted with a TextFormat instance.

```
1   class TextFieldExample extends MovieClip
2   {
3
4       public function TextFieldExample()
5       {
6           var txtField:TextField = this.createTextField(
    "txtField",1,100,100,100,100);
7           txtField.multiline = true;
8           txtField.wordWrap = true;
9           txtField.border = true;
10
11          var format:TextFormat = new TextFormat();
12          format.font = "Courier";
13
14          txtField.text = "A dynamically created text field";
15          txtField.setTextFormat(format);
16      }
17  }
```

> MovieClip was extended to create a text field dynamically.

> Use the text-field method setTextFormat to apply a TextFormat.

## AS3: Formatting

Text formatting with the TextFormat class is essentially the same in both versions of ActionScript. AS3 adds a few properties and changes the way you apply the format to a text field.

When you want to apply a text format to a text field, all you need to do is instantiate the TextFormat and apply the desired properties to the instance. Once you create the instance and set the properties, you use a new text-field method called defaultTextFormat to apply the format to the text field.

TextFormat is imported to
format the text field.

TextFormat is directly
instantiated to set the
text-field formatting.

defaultTextFormat
applies the properties set
on the format instance.

```
1   package
2   {
3       import flash.display.*;
4       import flash.text.TextField;
5       import flash.text.TextFieldAutoSize;
6       import flash.text.TextFormat;
7
8       public class TextFieldExample extends Sprite
9       {
10          private var label:TextField;
11          public function TextFieldExample()
12          {
13              this.createTextField();
14              this.setLabel();
15          }
16
17          private function setLabel():void
18          {
19              this.label.text = "Dynamic embedded font";
20          }
21
22          private function createTextField():void
23          {
24              this.label = new TextField();
25              this.label.autoSize = TextFieldAutoSize.LEFT;
26              this.label.background = true;
27              this.label.border = true;
28
29              var format:TextFormat = new TextFormat();
30              format.font = "Arial";
31              format.color = "0x000000";
32              format.size = 24;
33
34              this.label.defaultTextFormat = format;
35              addChild(this.label);
36          }
37      }
38  }
```

CHAPTER 8

# Buttons and MovieClips

Button AND MovieClip OBJECTS HAVE been completely over-
hauled in ActionScript 3. Both objects are now part of the display
list, inheriting properties, methods, and events from all display
classes in the inheritance chain. Buttons and MovieClips are
both InteractiveObjects, but it's important to keep in mind that
only the MovieClip class is a DisplayObjectContainer. In AS3 a
MovieClip is essentially a Sprite with a timeline, and the Button
class has been renamed and replaced with the SimpleButton class.

In this chapter, you will learn the differences between AS2 and
AS3 in how to handle mouse events, drag a movie clip, and work
with depth in the new display-list architecture.

# Mouse Events

Button and MovieClip symbol interactions are handled much differently in ActionScript 3 because of the new event-handling model. Callback-function properties ruled button and movie-clip interactions in AS2, but mouse events have taken over in AS3.

## AS2: Mouse Events

In AS2, button and movie-clip actions are handled through callback-function properties such as onRelease, onPress, and onReleaseOutside, just to name a few. These callback-function properties provide a way to handle user interaction.

The following example assumes that a movie clip has been added to the stage and has been linked to a class named MovieClipExample. The MovieClipExample uses the onRelease callback-function property to handle user interaction with a movie clip. The Delegate class passes the action to a custom class method, and the method controls what happens from there.

| | |
|---|---|
| Delegate is used to trigger a custom class method. | |

```
 1   import mx.utils.Delegate;
 2
 3   class MovieClipExample extends MovieClip
 4   {
 5
 6       public function MovieClipExample(Void)
 7       {
 8           this.onRelease = Delegate.create(this, onClick);
 9       }
10
11       private function onClick(Void):Void
12       {
13           trace("onClick");
14       }
15
16   }
```

Delegate is used to trigger a custom class method.

Delegate diverts the onRelease to a custom class method.

onClick is used as the callback function for the onRelease event.

## AS3: Mouse Events

Mouse events are integrated into the same event-handling architecture available to all event objects in ActionScript 3. The new architecture makes development much easier by providing one option, unlike the multiple options in AS2. This means you can finally rely on the same functionality for all events.

The following example shows how to add a listener to a movie clip and dispatch an event when the movie clip is clicked. The event is dispatched to a custom class method like that of the AS2 example, but the solution is more streamlined.

Another perk of the MouseEvent object is the event object that is passed to the class method. This event object contains detailed and extremely useful information about the movie clip that was clicked, such as the position, name, and so on.

```
 1  package
 2  {
 3      import flash.display.*;
 4      import flash.events.MouseEvent;
 5
 6      public class MovieClipExample extends MovieClip
 7      {
 8
 9          public function MovieClipExample()
10          {
11              this.addEventListener(MouseEvent.CLICK,
    this.onClick);
12          }
13
14          private function onClick(event:MouseEvent):void
15          {
16              trace("onClick: "+ event);
17          }
18
19      }
20  }
```

MouseEvent is imported to capture mouse events.

MovieClipExample listens for the CLICK event, which triggers the onClick method.

The MouseEvent, which is passed as a parameter to onClick, contains details about the event.

With ActionScript 3, you can create button symbols dynamically, which you could not do in AS2, because Button was a pseudo-class, which could only be created in the authoring environment. To do so, you must use a new class named SimpleButton. This class allows for the custom states to be created and assigned to the instance through public properties.

The following example shows how you can use this class to instantiate a SimpleButton and assign graphic shapes as the values of the properties. These custom shapes are then used as the different interaction states.

Once you create the button and add it to the movie, a MouseEvent can be applied.

```
1   package
2   {
3       import flash.display.*;
4       import flash.events.MouseEvent;
5
6       public class ButtonExample extends Sprite
7       {
8
9           public function ButtonExample()
10          {
11              var btn:SimpleButton = new SimpleButton();
12              btn.upState =
this.drawButtonState(0x000000, 100);
13              btn.overState =
this.drawButtonState(0xcccccc, 100);
14              btn.downState =
this.drawButtonState(0x000000, 100);
15              btn.hitTestState =
this.drawButtonState(0x000000, 100);
16              this.addChild(btn);
17              btn.addEventListener(MouseEvent.CLICK,
this.onClick);
18          }
19
20          private function drawButtonState(bgcolor:uint,
size:uint):DisplayObject
21          {
22              var shape:Sprite = new Sprite();
23              shape.graphics.beginFill(bgcolor);
24              shape.graphics.drawRect(0, 0, size, size);
25              shape.graphics.endFill();
26              return DisplayObject(shape);
27          }
28
29          private function onClick(event:MouseEvent):void
30          {
31              trace("onClick: "+ event);
32          }
33
34      }
35  }
```

SimpleButton is instantiated, and the different states of the button are assigned through a custom class method.

MouseEvent.CLICK is assigned to the button.

drawButtonState is used to create shapes based on a background color and size.

As with the MovieClipExample class, the onClick method is called when the button is clicked.

# Drag

Drag functionality is essential to understand when developing for Flash and ActionScript, specifically as it pertains to movie clips. Both ActionScript 2 and 3 offer drag functionality and include the same methods to handle it: startDrag and stopDrag. Although the methods are the same, the way dragging begins, progresses, and ends—in addition to the parameters that the startDrag method accepts—have all changed in AS3.

Drag functionality always includes a beginning, a middle, and an end. The beginning is the initial selection of the item, which triggers the dragging; the middle is the actual dragging process; and the end is when the dragged item is released. Here's how each of these steps can contain its own functionality:

1. The beginning contains code to initiate the dragging action, usually upon clicking the draggable item.

2. The middle contains functionality to determine whether a target has been reached with the draggable item.

3. The end contains code that occurs when the draggable item is released.

Let's take a look at how drag functionality differs with the changes in the startDrag method and the integration of events in ActionScript.

## AS2: Drag

Dragging a movie clip in ActionScript 2 consists of the steps mentioned above combined with the onPress, onRelease, and onReleaseOuside callback-function properties.

The following example assumes a movie-clip symbol with a linked DragExample class exists on the stage of a Flash movie, and that the movie-clip symbol contains an embedded movie-clip instance called mc. The dragging starts with a mouse press on the movie-clip instance called mc, and ends when the mouse releases the movie clip. If the mouse happens not to be directly over the movie clip at the time of release, onReleaseOutside catches the event.

```
1   import mx.utils.Delegate;
2
3   class DragExample extends MovieClip
4   {
5       private var mc:MovieClip;
6
```

mc is an embedded movie clip in the movie clip that is linked to the DragExample class.

```
 7        public function DragExample(Void)
 8        {
 9            this.mc.onPress =
     Delegate.create(this, startDragItem);
10            this.mc.onRelease = this.mc.onReleaseOutside =
     Delegate.create(this, stopDragItem);
11        }
12
13        private function startDragItem(Void):Void
14        {
15            trace("Start dragging");
16            this.mc.startDrag();
17        }
18
19        private function stopDragItem(Void):Void
20        {
21            trace("Stop dragging");
22            trace("-------");
23            this.mc.stopDrag();
24        }
25 }
```

When mc is pressed, the dragging initiates.

When mc is released or there is a release outside of mc, the dragging stops.

startDragItem starts the dragging. If no arguments are passed to the startDrag method, the draggable item has no bounds.

stopDragItem stops the dragging when the draggable item is released.

The drag functionality itself isn't very complicated, but what if you want to execute code while an item is being dragged? One trick to accomplish this is the onEnterFrame callback-function property. When the dragging is initiated, an onEnterFrame is also initiated to continually call a class method that executes code while the item is dragged. Then, to remove the drag functionality, you simply set the onEnterFrame to null when the item is released.

```
 1 import mx.utils.Delegate;
 2
 3 class DragExample extends MovieClip
 4 {
 5     private var mc:MovieClip;
 6
 7     public function DragExample(Void)
 8     {
 9         this.mc.onPress =
     Delegate.create(this, startDragItem);
10         this.mc.onRelease = this.mc.onReleaseOutside =
     Delegate.create(this, stopDragItem);
11     }
12
```

| | |
|---|---|
| startDrag can also receive the lockcenter, x, y, width, and height arguments. | |
| onEnterFrame executes a class method called onDragItem continuously. | |
| onDragItem continually executes when the onEnterFrame callback-function property is running. | |
| onEnterFrame is set to null to stop the execution of onDragItem. | |

```
13    private function startDragItem(Void):Void
14    {
15        trace("Start dragging");
16        this.mc.startDrag(false, 0, 0, 200, 200);
17        this.mc.onEnterFrame =
      Delegate.create(this, onDragItem);
18    }
19
20    private function onDragItem(Void):Void
21    {
22        trace("Dragging");
23    }
24
25    private function stopDragItem(Void):Void
26    {
27        trace("Stop dragging");
28        trace("-------");
29        this.mc.stopDrag();
30        this.mc.onEnterFrame = null;
31    }
32 }
```

## AS3: Drag

startDrag and stopDrag are no longer direct methods of the MovieClip class. Instead they are inherited from the Sprite class. This means that both sprites and movie clips can use this functionality. If you need to contain a timeline in the draggable item, use a movie clip. Otherwise you would use a sprite.

The following example shows how to use the MouseEvent class to control dragging a movie clip named mc. The example assumes that the mc movie-clip instance has been added to the stage, and that the DragExample class is the document class.

| | |
|---|---|
| MouseEvent is imported to provide mouse events to the class. | |
| currentDraggable will store a reference to a dragged item. | |

```
1 package
2 {
3     import flash.display.*;
4     import flash.events.MouseEvent;
5
6     public class DragExample extends Sprite
7     {
8         private var currentDraggable:Sprite;
```

| | |
|---|---|
| When the MOUSE_DOWN event is triggered, startDragItem executes code to initiate the dragging. | 9 10 11 12 |
| currentDraggable is determined based on the event object's currentTarget. | 13 14 15 16 17 18 |
| The dragging begins without any bounds. | 19 |
| The MOUSE_MOVE event is used instead of onEnterFrame. The stage is used because mouse movement must be tracked over the entire movie, not a specific movie clip. | 20 21 22 23 24 25 |
| MOUSE_UP event replaces onRelease and onReleaseOutside by firing when the mouse is released anywhere over the stage. | 26 27 28 29 30 |
| The listeners are removed from the stage, and the dragging is stopped with the stopDrag method. | 31 32 33 34 35 36 37 38 39 |

```
        public function DragExample(Void)
        {
            this.mc.addEventListener(MouseEvent.MOUSE_DOWN,
startDragItem);
        }

        private function startDragItem(event:MouseEvent):void
        {
            trace("Start dragging");
            this.currentDraggable =
Sprite(event.currentTarget);
            this.currentDraggable.startDrag();

            stage.addEventListener(MouseEvent.MOUSE_MOVE,
onDragItem);
        }

        private function onDragItem(event:MouseEvent):void
        {
            trace("Dragging");
            stage.addEventListener(MouseEvent.MOUSE_UP,
stopDragItem);
        }

        private function stopDragItem(event:MouseEvent):void
        {
            trace("Stop dragging",
                "\n--------");
            stage.removeEventListener(MouseEvent.MOUSE_MOVE,
onDragItem);
            stage.removeEventListener(MouseEvent.MOUSE_UP,
stopDragItem);
            this.currentDraggable.stopDrag();
        }
    }

}
```

If you want to control the area where the movie clip could be dragged, you cannot simply add numbers to the startDrag method as you could in AS2. In AS3 you must use a new class named Rectangle as the second parameter for the startDrag method to define the bounds in which the item can be dragged. Luckily, the Rectangle class is easy to use; all you need to do is instantiate the class and pass the *x, y,* width and height numbers that you would have passed directly to the startDrag method in AS2. In the previous example, you would simply modify code line 19 to the following:

```
19   this.currentDraggable.startDrag(false, new Rectangle(0, 0,
     200, 200));
```

# Depth

Depth control is another important piece of functionality in Flash. Depth determines how items are visually arranged in three-dimensional space in a Flash movie, and it is a very important factor when creating drag functionality. The differences between AS2 and AS3 in how depth is handled are major because of the new display-list structure.

## AS2: Depth

Depth control in ActionScript 2 is as easy as specifying the depth number in which you want a movie clip to reside, or swapping depths with another item in the Flash movie.

The following code is an addition to the dragging sample. The example uses the MovieClip classes' swapDepths and getNextHighestDepth methods to position the draggable movie clip in front of all other items when the dragging initiates.

Remember that this sample assumes you have a movie-clip instance embedded in the item linked to the DragExample class.

```
1   import mx.utils.Delegate;
2
3   class DragExample extends MovieClip
4   {
5       private var mc:MovieClip;
6
7       public function DragExample(Void)
8       {
9           this.mc.onPress = Delegate.create(this,
    startDragItem);
```

```
10              this.mc.onRelease = this.mc.onReleaseOutside =
        Delegate.create(this, stopDragItem);
11          }
12
13      private function startDragItem(Void):Void
14      {
15          this.mc.startDrag();
16          this.mc.swapDepths(this.getNextHighestDepth());
17      }
18
19      private function stopDragItem(Void):Void
20      {
21          this.mc.stopDrag();
22      }
23  }
```

swapDepths is used to arrange the mc in front of all other elements in the Flash movie.

## AS3: Depth

Because of the new display architecture, depth control in ActionScript 3 is much different than it was in AS2. AS3 does not include the swapDepths and getNextHighestDepth methods. The functionality is still possible, but you need to write custom code to create the same effect.

In the following example, when dragging initiates in AS3, the parent object is accessed to determine how many child items exist. To simulate the functionality you would have received from the getNextHighestDepth in AS2, you can use the number of children in the parent object to set the child index on the item, which you want to bring to the front.

NOTE The number of children comes back as an array through the numChildren property. Because arrays start with 0, the numChildren count must subtract one to get an accurate number.

```
1   package
2   {
3       import flash.display.*;
4       import flash.events.MouseEvent;
5
6       public class DragExample extends Sprite
7       {
8           private var currentDraggable:Sprite;
9
10          public function DragExample()
11          {
12              this.mc.addEventListener(MouseEvent.MOUSE_DOWN,
        startDragItem);
13          }
```

```
14
15          private function startDragItem(event:MouseEvent):void
16          {
17              this.currentDraggable =
        Sprite(event.currentTarget);
18              this.currentDraggable.startDrag();
19              stage.addEventListener(MouseEvent.MOUSE_UP,
        stopDragItem);
20                  this.setChildIndex(this.currentDraggable,
        this.numChildren-1);
21          }
22
23          private function stopDragItem(event:MouseEvent):void
24          {
25              stage.removeEventListener(MouseEvent.MOUSE_UP,
        stopDragItem);
26              this.currentDraggable.stopDrag();
27          }
28      }
29
30 }
```

setChildIndex is used to arrange currentDraggable in front of all other elements in the parent display object.

CHAPTER 9

# Loading

LOADING EXTERNAL ASSETS has provided Flash with completely dynamic functionality, allowing XML and database connectivity, and image and movie display. This chapter covers the differences between ActionScript 2 and ActionScript 3 in how to load external variables, how to trigger a URL to a Web site, and how to load external assets and track their progress with ActionScript.

# Loading External Variables

Loading external variables in ActionScript is made possible with the flashvars attribute and/or tag, depending on the implementation. Flashvars offers a direct method for passing name-value pairs to a Flash movie through embed and object tags. While the process of passing variables to a Flash movie is virtually the same in both versions of ActionScript, the retrieval methods have changed.

## AS2: Loading External Variables

In ActionScript 2, external variables can be passed to a Flash movie through the embed and object tags using flashvars. The HTML that displays Flash movies contains two versions of flashvars; which version is used depends on the type of browser that is rendering the movie. Internet Explorer uses the object tag, which requires an additional flashvars param tag with name-value pairs as the value. Mozilla Firefox and Apple Safari use the embed tag, which requires an additional attribute in the embed tag called flashvars with name-value pairs as the value.

In the following example, the object and embed code contains the appropriate flashvars to pass a variable called uid, as a unique id that has a value of 1.

```
1  <object classid="clsid:d27cdb6e-ae6d-11cf-96b8-444553540000"
2          codebase="http://download.macromedia.com/pub/
   shockwave/cabs/flash/swflash.cab#version=8,0,0,0"
3          width="100"
4          height="100"
5          id="movieId">
6
7      <param name="allowScriptAccess" value="sameDomain" />
8      <param name="allowFullScreen" value="false" />
9      <param name="movie" value="path/file.swf" />
10     <param name="quality" value="high" />
11     <param name="flashvars" value="uid=1" />
12
13     <embed src="path/file.swf"
14         flashvars="uid=1"
15         quality="high"
16         width="100"
17         height="100"
18         name="movieId"
```

flashvars is assigned a value in a param tag for browsers that use the object tag.

flashvars is assigned a value in the embed tag for Firefox and Safari.

```
19        allowScriptAccess="sameDomain"
20        allowFullScreen="false"
21        type="application/x-shockwave-flash"
22        pluginspage="http://www.macromedia.com/go/
   getflashplayer" />
23    </object>
```

Retrieving the value of the uid variable is simple in AS2, as name-value pairs from flashvars are automatically converted to properties of _root. Therefore, the uid property is available via the _root in the following example.

<table>
<tr><td>

All name-value pairs assigned to flashvars are available by name via _root.

</td><td>

```
1  class ExternalVarExample extends MovieClip
2  {
3      public function ExternalVarExample(Void)
4      {
5          trace("uid: "+ _root.uid);
6      }
7  }
```

</td></tr>
</table>

## AS3: Loading External Variables

ActionScript 3 doesn't handle flashvars any differently in the HTML code for a Flash movie, but Flash Player 9 or above does require small changes to the code used in the previous example.

<table>
<tr><td>

The player version corresponds to the player required to play the movie.

</td><td>

```
1  <object classid="clsid:d27cdb6e-ae6d-11cf-96b8-444553540000"
2      codebase="http://download.macromedia.com/pub/shockwave/
   cabs/flash/swflash.cab#version=9,0,0,0"
3      width="100"
4      height="100"
5      id="movieId">
6
7      <param name="allowScriptAccess" value="sameDomain" />
8      <param name="allowFullScreen" value="false" />
9      <param name="movie" value="path/file.swf"  />
10     <param name="quality" value="high" />
11     <param name="flashvars" value="uid=1">
12
13     <embed src="path/file.swf"
14         flashvars="uid=1"
15         quality="high"
16         width="100"
17         height="100"
```

</td></tr>
</table>

<table>
<tr><td>

flashvars is assigned a value in a param tag for browsers that use the object tag.

</td></tr>
<tr><td>

The flashvars property is assigned a value in the embed tag for Firefox and Safari.

</td></tr>
</table>

```
18          name="movieId"
19          allowScriptAccess="sameDomain"
20          allowFullScreen="false"
21          type="application/x-shockwave-flash"
22          pluginspage="http://www.macromedia.com/go/
    getflashplayer" />
23    </object>
```

The major difference in how flashvars are handled is in the retrieval of the variables. While the root is still used to retrieve the variables passed through flashvars, the variables are not directly accessible.

In AS3, all DisplayObjects have a property named loaderInfo, which is essentially a LoaderInfo object. Because root is a DisplayObject, the loaderInfo property can be used to retrieve loading information about the root.

In the following example, the loaderInfo property is used to access the parameters in the LoaderInfo object. Those parameters correspond to the name-value pairs made available via flashvars.

```
1   package
2   {
3       import flash.display.*;
4
5       public class ExternalVarExample extends Sprite
6       {
7           public function ExternalVarExample()
8           {
9               trace("uid: "+ root.loaderInfo.parameters.uid);
10          }
11      }
12  }
```

All name-value pairs assigned to flashvars are available by name as parameters of the loaderInfo property of the root object.

# Triggering a URL

Like HTML, ActionScript offers ways to launch external URLs, and define a target window and a request method. The concept is the same in both versions of ActionScript, but AS3 offers a more robust solution defined by objects rather than simple strings.

## AS2: Triggering a URL

ActionScript 2 provides a function called getURL that lets you launch an external URL. Because getURL is a global function, it is accessible to all classes.

In the following example, a custom class is used to redirect the user to a URL via the getURL function.

getURL launches the specified URL.

```
1  class GetUrlExample extends MovieClip
2  {
3      public function GetUrlExample()
4      {
5          _root.getURL("http://www.peachpit.com");
6      }
7  }
```

To launch the URL in a new window, you would use the following code.

getURL launches the specified URL in a new window.

```
1  class GetUrlExample extends MovieClip
2  {
3      public function GetUrlExample()
4      {
5          _root.getURL("http://www.peachpit.com", "_blank");
6      }
7  }
```

Actual ActionScript variables must be created before you can send variables via the GET or POST methods and the getURL function is called. In the following example, the firstName and lastName variables are passed to the URL via the POST method.

getURL sends the firstName and lastName name-value pairs via the POST method to the specified URL.

```
1  class GetUrlExample extends MovieClip
2  {
3      public function GetUrlExample()
4      {
5          var firstName:String = "Kris";
6          var lastName:String = "Hadlock";
7          _root.getURL("http://www.peachpit.com", "_blank",
   "POST");
8      }
9  }
```

## AS3: Triggering a URL

ActionScript 3 has a new way to call an external URL and send variables. A new function called navigateToURL has taken the place of the global getURL function. It is available by importing the flash.net package. Rather than taking a string parameter as the URL, an actual object must be passed to the navigateToURL function as a URLRequest object. (The navigateToURL function is also available via the flash.net package.) The URLRequest object is a more robust solution than what ActionScript 2 provided, as the class offers numerous properties such as url, contentType, data, method, and requestHeaders.

In the following example, a simple URLRequest object is instantiated and passed to the navigateToURL function, which redirects the user to the specified URL.

The flash.net package is imported to access the URLRequest object and navigateToURL function.

URLRequest directs the URL to launch via the navigateToURL function.

```
1  package
2  {
3      import flash.display.*;
4      import flash.net.*;
5
6      public class NavigateToUrlExample extends Sprite
7      {
8          public function NavigateToUrlExample()
9          {
10             var req:URLRequest =
new URLRequest("http://www.peachpit.com");
11             navigateToURL(req);
12         }
13     }
14 }
```

If you want to target a new window, the target is passed as a string as the second parameter of the navigateToURL function.

The flash.net package is imported to access the URLRequest object and navigateToURL function.

```
1  package
2  {
3      import flash.display.*;
4      import flash.net.*;
5
6      public class NavigateToUrlExample extends Sprite
7      {
8          public function NavigateToUrlExample()
9          {
```

```
10          var req:URLRequest =
new URLRequest("http://www.peachpit.com");
11              navigateToURL(req, "_blank");
12          }
13      }
14  }
```

The target window is passed as the second parameter as a string.

If variables need to be passed, you can use the method property of the URLRequest object. The method property takes a string value of GET, which is the default value, or POST.

Of course variables are not sent the same way as in AS2. You have to use another object called URLVariables, also available via the flash.net package, to define the variables that are sent through a URLRequest. A URLVariables object must first be instantiated, then variables can be applied to the object with values that you define. When all variables are created, they are assigned to the data property of the URLRequest being used.

In the following example, the URLVariables object is used to assign variables, which will be passed as name-value pairs through the POST method of the URLRequest object.

```
1   package
2   {
3       import flash.display.*;
4       import flash.net.*;
5
6       public class URLVariablesExample extends Sprite
7       {
8           public function URLVariablesExample()
9           {
10              var req:URLRequest =
new URLRequest("http://www.peachpit.com");
11              var variables:URLVariables = new URLVariables();
12              variables.firstName = "Kris";
13              variables.lastName = "Hadlock";
14
                req.data = variables;
15
                req.method = "POST";
16               navigateToURL(req);
17          }
18      }
19  }
```

The flash.net package is imported to access the URLRequest object, URLVariables object, and navigateToURL function.

URLVariables is used to store custom variables to be sent via a URLRequest.

URLVariables are assigned to the data property of the URLRequest.

POST is set as the method for the request.

# Loading External Assets

Flash's ability to load external movies, images, sound, and video has allowed it to officially compete with other dynamic platforms. With the new event-handling model and completely object-oriented ActionScript architecture, the way you load external assets is new, improved, and more controllable.

## AS2: Loading External Assets

The ability to load external assets in Flash provides a lot of power to developers, especially when loading external Flash movies. The most common way to load external flash movies with AS2 is through the MovieClipLoader class. This class provides inherent events to determine when a file has completed loading. Listeners can also be added to MovieClipLoader events to trigger custom class methods.

In the following example, the MovieClipLoader is instantiated, a listener is added, and an external Flash movie is loaded. When the Flash movie has finished loading, a custom class method is called and a reference to the MovieClip that contains the loaded movie is passed as a parameter.

MovieClipLoader is instantiated, and a listener is added to the class to trigger the onLoadComplete method when loading is done.

onLoadComplete is an inherit MovieClipLoader event that fires when loading completes.

```
1   class MovieClipLoaderExample extends MovieClip
2   {
3       private var mcl:MovieClipLoader;
4
5       public function MovieClipLoaderExample(Void)
6       {
7           this.mcl = new MovieClipLoader();
8           this.mcl.addListener(this);
9           var container:MovieClip =
    MovieClip(this.createEmptyMovieClip("container", 1));
10          this.mcl.loadClip("path/file.swf", container);
11      }
12
13      private function onLoadComplete(mc:MovieClip):Void
14      {
15          trace("onLoadComplete");
16      }
17  }
```

# AS3: Loading External Assets

ActionScript 3 provides more detail about externally loaded files and allows for more control of the loading process. As with other requests to external URLs, the URLRequest class must be used to create a request object for the particular file you want to load.

To initialize a file load, you instantiate a class called Loader, which is used to load external SWF and image files, and pass the URLRequest to its load method. The Loader class provides a property called contentLoaderInfo, which is a LoaderInfo object. An event listener is then added to the contentLoaderInfo property to determine when a file has completed loading. Once a file loads, the file is considered a DisplayObject and can be added as a child to the current DisplayObject.

URLRequest is imported to create a request for the file being loaded.

The flash.events package is imported to trigger loading events.

The Loader class is instantiated, and a URLRequest is passed to the load method to load a Flash movie.

contentLoaderInfo triggers EVENT.COMPLETE when a movie is done loading.

The onMovieLoaded method is called when the Flash movie is done loading. The loaded content is then targeted and added to the current DisplayObject.

```
1   package
2   {
3       import flash.display.*;
4       import flash.net.URLRequest;
5       import flash.events.*;
6
7       public class MovieClipLoaderExample extends Sprite
8       {
9           public function MovieClipLoaderExample()
10          {
11              var loader:Loader = new Loader();
12              loader.load(new URLRequest("path/file.swf"));
13              loader.contentLoaderInfo.addEventListener(
    Event.COMPLETE, onMovieLoaded);
14          }
15
16          private function onMovieLoaded(event:Event):void
17          {
18              var movie:Sprite = event.target.content;
19              addChild(movie);
20          }
21      }
22  }
```

# Tracking Load Progress

Since files come in all shapes and sizes, an important part of loading external assets is providing feedback to users about the progress of a loading file. Fortunately, both ActionScript 2 and 3 provide variables that you can use to determine how many bytes of a file have loaded and the file's total bytes.

## AS2: Tracking Load Progress

Tracking load progress in ActionScript 2 works just like using the onLoadComplete event to determine when a file has completed loading. The MovieClipLoader object has an inherent event called onLoadProgress, which is automatically triggered while a file is being loaded. The onLoadProgress event contains all the parameter variables necessary to provide feedback about the loading process, such as the container movie clip that the asset was loading into, the amount of bytes loaded, and the total bytes of the external asset.

```
1   class MovieClipLoaderExample extends MovieClip
2   {
3       private var mcl:MovieClipLoader;
4
5       public function MovieClipLoaderExample(Void)
6       {
7           this.mcl = new MovieClipLoader();
8           this.mcl.addListener(this);
9           var container:MovieClip =
    MovieClip(this.createEmptyMovieClip("container", 1));
10          this.mcl.loadClip("path/file.swf", container);
11      }
12
13      private function onLoadProgress(mc:MovieClip,
    loaded:Number, total:Number):Void
14      {
15          trace("onLoadProgress");
16      }
17
18      private function onLoadComplete(mc:MovieClip):Void
19      {
20          trace("onLoadComplete");
21      }
22  }
```

onLoadProgress is an inherited MovieClipLoader event used in the loading process.

# AS3: Tracking Load Progress

Tracking the loading progress of a file with ActionScript 3 requires a new event class called ProgressEvent. The ProgressEvent class contains an event called PROGRESS, which can be used in an event listener to trigger a custom class method. The custom class method that is triggered by the PROGRESS event receives all the variables necessary to display progress to a user in a ProgressEvent object that is passed as a parameter. The two important properties that the ProgressEvent parameter includes for determining progress are bytesLoaded and bytesTotal.

```
 1  package
 2  {
 3      import flash.display.*;
 4      import flash.net.URLRequest;
 5      import flash.events.*;
 6
 7      public class MovieClipLoaderExample extends Sprite
 8      {
 9          public function MovieClipLoaderExample()
10          {
11              var loader:Loader = new Loader();
12              loader.load(new URLRequest("path/file.swf"));
13              loader.contentLoaderInfo.addEventListener(
    Event.COMPLETE, onMovieLoaded);
14              loader.contentLoaderInfo.addEventListener(
    ProgressEvent.PROGRESS, onProgress);
15          }
16
17          private function onProgress(event:ProgressEvent):void
18          {
19              trace("Loaded: "+ event.bytesLoaded, "Total: "+
    event.bytesTotal);
20          }
21
22          private function onMovieLoaded(event:Event):void
23          {
24              var movie:Sprite = event.target.content;
25              addChild(movie);
26          }
27      }
28  }
```

onProgress is the custom method that is called during the loading process set by ProgressEvent.PROGRESS.

# 10

# XML

XML IS AN IMPORTANT PART of dynamic ActionScript development, as it provides ways to define external data and simplify your ActionScript code. You can update XML content in a published Flash movie without republishing the Flash movie. XML data can also be dynamic, possibly even written based on database values.

With each new version of ActionScript, the XML object has been improved. While it existed in the original version of ActionScript, ActionScript 2 made it a native object. Now in ActionScript 3, the ECMAScript for XML (E4X) specification has been implemented, marking a giant step forward. E4X makes XML development consistent with the rest of the ActionScript syntax, providing a way to implement common operators, such as the dot (.) operator, to manipulate data.

ActionScript follows the ECMAScript for XML specification with the combination of the XML, XMLList, QName, and Namespace classes collectively known as E4X. This chapter covers some of the differences between the AS2 and AS3 versions of the XML object for tasks such as loading, event handling, and parsing.

# Loading and Events

The XML object in ActionScript 2 is now equivalent to ActionScript 3's XMLDocument. Those two are used in exactly the same way, so I won't cover them here. Instead, this section focuses on the new ways you can use XML, and the differences between the old and new versions of the XML object.

Most of the time, using XML involves using external files that allow custom updates to be made to a published SWF file. The following code is an example of an XML file; we will load it to both ActionScript examples.

> **NOTE** employees is the root element. Numerous employee elements can exist as child elements. Text data within CDATA is not parsed by the XML parser and is used to prevent issues with special characters.

```
1  <employees>
2      <employee>
3          <firstName><![CDATA[Jane]]></firstName>
4          <lastName><![CDATA[Doe]]></lastName>
5      </employee>
6  </employees>
```

## AS2: Loading and Events

In order for ActionScript to parse the data in an external XML document, the file must be represented as an XML object. Loading can proceed once an XML object has been instantiated, but make sure to ignore the white space in the document to prevent parsing issues.

The loading process begins with the load function, where you specify the path to the XML file that you want to load. In order to decipher when the XML file has loaded, the onLoad callback function is used. When used in a class, the onLoad function can use the Delegate to pass the event to a custom class method.

```
1   import mx.utils.Delegate;
2   class XMLLoadingExample extends MovieClip
3   {
4       private var _xml:XML;
5
6       public function XMLLoadingExample(Void)
7       {
8           this._xml = new XML();
9           this._xml.ignoreWhite = true;
10          this._xml.load("path/file.xml");
11          this._xml.onLoad = Delegate.create(this,
    onXMLLoaded);
12      }
13
14      private function onXMLLoaded(Void):Void
15      {
16          trace("XML Loaded: "+ this._xml);
17      }
18  }
```

_xml is available throughout the class.

The XML object is instantiated and the document's white space is ignored.

load specifies the path to the XML file. The onLoad event is passed to a custom class method through the Delegate.

onXMLLoaded is used as the callback when the XML file is done loading.

## AS3: Loading and Events

ActionScript 3's XML object functions much differently than that of ActionScript 2. In AS3, an XML file must be officially loaded before the data can even be cast as (or converted to) an XML object.

The following code uses the same employee XML file sample, but the process of loading the file and passing the events is completely different. As covered in Chapter 9, loading is no longer handled by individual objects. Instead, all loading is handled by the URLLoader and URLRequest classes from the flash.net package. In order to initiate the loading of an XML file, the URLLoader must be instantiated, and a URLRequest must be passed to the load method of the URLLoader, to specify the path to the file being loaded. Event listeners are then added to dispatch custom class methods when different events occur, such as the loading progress or completion of an XML file.

In the example below, a custom class method named onXMLLoaded catches the completion event of the XML file. When onXMLLoaded is called, the event object that dispatched the method is passed as a parameter. This event is then used to retrieve the event target, which in this case is the URLLoader.

Finally, the XML object can be instantiated based on the data contained in the URLLoader object.

In essence, this is the only time the XML object is used in this entire example; the rest of the code is all built around the loading process. The benefit of this approach is that the XML object is completely separated from the loading process, thus simplifying the code.

```
1   package
2   {
3       import flash.display.*;
4       import flash.net.URLLoader;
5       import flash.net.URLRequest;
6       import flash.xml.*;
7       import flash.events.*;
8
9       public class XMLLoadingExample extends Sprite
10      {
11          public function XMLLoadingExample()
12          {
13              var uLoader:URLLoader = new URLLoader();
14              uLoader.addEventListener(ProgressEvent.PROGRESS,
    onXMLProgress);
15              uLoader.addEventListener(Event.COMPLETE,
    onXMLLoaded);
16              uLoader.load(new URLRequest("path/file.xml"));
17          }
18
19          private function onXMLProgress(
    event:ProgressEvent):void
20          {
21              trace("Loaded: " + event.bytesLoaded, "Total: "
    + event.bytesTotal);
22          }
23
24          private function onXMLLoaded(event:Event):void
25          {
26              var loader:URLLoader = URLLoader(event.target);
27              var _xml:XML = new XML(loader.data);
28          }
29      }
30  }
```

The URLLoader loads the URLRequest to the XML file and dispatches a PROGRESS and COMPLETE event.

The onXMLLoaded method is called when the XML file is completely loaded. The event object is used to determine the target and then the data that was loaded.

# Parsing

Parsing XML has always involved a lot of code writing to target appropriate nodes, attributes, and values. At last, ActionScript 3 has alleviated the pain of having to write so much code.

The following code serves as the XML file sample for both ActionScript examples in this section. The XML file has been updated to include multiple employees, each of which has an attribute for an id associated with his or her name.

Each employee now has an id attribute.

```
1  <employees>
2      <employee id="1234">
3          <firstName><![CDATA[Jane]]></firstName>
4          <lastName><![CDATA[Doe]]></lastName>
5      </employee>
6      <employee id="5678">
7          <firstName><![CDATA[John]]></firstName>
8          <lastName><![CDATA[Doe]]></lastName>
9      </employee>
10 </employees>
```

## AS2: Parsing

As mentioned, parsing XML with ActionScript has always been a little tedious. The code in this example uses AS2 to parse the XML object when the XML file is completely loaded. In order to retrieve the few data items from the XML file, the employees element needs to be targeted and typed as an Array, then the Array of employees is iterated to target the id attribute. Within the first loop each employee element must be converted into an Array of its childNodes, and a second loop must be used to iterate the first and last name of each employee.

```
1  import mx.utils.Delegate;
2  class XMLLoadingExample extends MovieClip
3  {
4      private var _xml:XML;
5
6      public function XMLLoadingExample(Void)
7      {
8          this._xml = new XML();
9          this._xml.ignoreWhite = true;
10         this._xml.load("path/file.xml");
```

| | |
|---|---|
| 11 | `        this._xml.onLoad = Delegate.create(this,` |
| | `onXMLLoaded);` |
| 12 | `    }` |
| 13 | |
| 14 | `    private function onXMLLoaded(Void):Void` |
| 15 | `    {` |
| 16 | `        var employees:Array =` |
| | `this._xml.firstChild.childNodes;` |
| 17 | `        for(var i:Number=0; i<employees.length; i++)` |
| 18 | `        {` |
| 19 | `            trace("id: "+ employees[i].attributes.id);` |
| 20 | |
| 21 | `            var employee:Array = employees[i].childNodes;` |
| 22 | `            for(var j:Number=0; j<employee.length; j++)` |
| 23 | `            {` |
| 24 | `                switch(employee[j].nodeName)` |
| 25 | `                {` |
| 26 | `                    case "firstName":` |
| 27 | `                        trace("firstName: "+` |
| | `employee[j].firstChild.nodeValue);` |
| 28 | `                        break;` |
| 29 | `                    case "lastName":` |
| 30 | `                        trace("lastName: "+` |
| | `employee[j].firstChild.nodeValue);` |
| 31 | `                        break;` |
| 32 | `                    default:` |
| 33 | `                }` |
| 34 | `            }` |
| 35 | `            trace("----");` |
| 36 | `        }` |
| 37 | `    }` |
| 38 | `}` |

Side notes:

- With the XML loaded, the employees are targeted as an Array.
- The employees Array is iterated.
- The attributes property targets the id.
- Each employee is split into an Array and iterated.
- Determine what node value is being accessed.

## AS3: Parsing

AS3's E4X makes XML parsing extremely easy, and far less code is needed to access specific values. In the following example, the dot (.) and attribute identifier (@) operators are used to target the elements and attributes in the XML object as if each element and attribute were native. Also, rather than using an Array to represent the employees, AS3 uses the XMLList class, which provides more methods that are not available to Array instances.

```
1   package
2   {
3       import flash.display.*;
4       import flash.net.URLLoader;
5       import flash.net.URLRequest;
6       import flash.xml.*;
7       import flash.events.*;
8
9       public class XMLLoadingExample extends Sprite
10      {
11          public function XMLLoadingExample()
12          {
13              var uLoader:URLLoader = new URLLoader();
14              uLoader.addEventListener(ProgressEvent.PROGRESS,
    onXMLProgress);
15              uLoader.addEventListener(Event.COMPLETE,
    onXMLLoaded);
16              uLoader.load(new URLRequest("path/file.xml"));
17          }
18
19          private function onXMLProgress(
    event:ProgressEvent):void
20          {
21              trace("Loaded: "+ event.bytesLoaded, "Total: "+
    event.bytesTotal);
22          }
23
24          private function onXMLLoaded(event:Event):void
25          {
26              var loader:URLLoader = URLLoader(event.target);
27              var _xml:XML = new XML(loader.data);
28
29              var employees:XMLList = _xml..employee;
30              for each(var employee:XML in employees)
31              {
32              trace("id: "+ employee.@id.toString(),
                  "\nfirstName: "+ employee.firstName.toString(),
                  "\nlastName: "+ employee.lastName.toString(),
                  "\n----");
33              }
34          }
35      }
36  }
```

The employees are represented as an XMLList rather than an Array.

Each employee is iterated, and the dot (.) and attribute (@) operators target the appropriate values.

CHAPTER **11**

# Drawing and Color

DYNAMICALLY DRAWING SHAPES, lines, and even graphs with the Drawing API is one of the benefits of using ActionScript. Add color and gradients to the list and there are no limits.

This chapter covers the major renovations that have occurred in the ActionScript Drawing API and new ways to apply color transformations.

# Lines

Borders, graphs, and outlines are just a few of the graphics that can be drawn using lines. Lines are essentially the same in ActionScript 2 and 3, including joint and caps styles, a line scale mode, color, and size. However, while the lines are the same, the way they are created has been updated to a more object-oriented approach.

## AS2: Lines

ActionScript 2 includes drawing in the MovieClip class. The MovieClip class controls fills, shapes, lines, and any other drawing functionality. The main functions for drawing lines are lineStyle, moveTo, and lineTo. The lineStyle function defines how the finished line will appear, defining size, color, alpha, and so on. The moveTo function moves the drawing tool to point-locations on the x-axis and y-axis without actually drawing anything. The actual drawing begins with the lineTo function, which defines what point-locations on the x- and y-axis to use for drawing each piece of a graphic. The LineExample class shows how to draw a simple triangle with lines.

A movie clip is necessary when drawing.

lineStyle defines the final appearance of the line. moveTo defines the starting point of the line. The lineTo functions define the end shape.

```
1  class LineExample extends MovieClip
2  {
3      public function LineExample(Void)
4      {
5          var triangleHeight:Number = 100;
6          var triangle:MovieClip =
   MovieClip(this.createEmptyMovieClip("triangle", 1));
7
8          triangle.lineStyle(10, 0xcccccc, 100, false,
   "vertical", "none", "miter", 10);
9          triangle.moveTo(triangleHeight/2, 0);
10         triangle.lineTo(triangleHeight, triangleHeight);
11         triangle.lineTo(0, triangleHeight);
12         triangle.lineTo(triangleHeight/2, 0);
13     }
14 }
```

## AS3: Lines

In ActionScript 3, drawing no longer depends on the MovieClip class. Instead, the Graphics class is used to create all vector shapes. However, the

Sprite or Shape class must be used to create a graphic, as the Graphic class cannot be instantiated independently.

In order to draw using the Sprite or Shape class, you use the graphics property. The graphics property references a Graphics object that includes all the methods and properties necessary to draw shapes, lines, and so on.

Other improvements include the LineScaleMode, JointStyle, and CapsStyle classes. Each of these classes contains static properties that provide the values for their specific function. For example, JointStyle provides static BEVEL, MITER, and ROUND properties used to define a line's joint style. The benefit of this object-oriented approach is you can rely on static properties rather than string values. For example, instead of using the string "miter" as a parameter value in the lineStyle function, JointStyle.MITER is used.

Static classes define the appearance of a line.

Import Shape to create a graphic.

Shape is instantiated to target graphics.

The lineStyle function is much cleaner with static classes to define values. The graphics property is the way to draw with AS3.

The Shape instance is added to the movie.

```
1   package
2   {
3       import flash.display.Sprite;
4       import flash.display.LineScaleMode;
5       import flash.display.CapsStyle;
6       import flash.display.JointStyle;
7       import flash.display.Shape;
8
9       public class LineExample extends Sprite
10      {
11          public function LineExample()
12          {
13              var triangleHeight:uint = 100;
14              var triangle:Shape = new Shape();
15              triangle.graphics.lineStyle(10, 0xcccccc, 1,
    false, LineScaleMode.VERTICAL, CapsStyle.NONE, JointStyle.MITER,
    10);
16              triangle.graphics.moveTo(triangleHeight/2, 0);
17              triangle.graphics.lineTo(triangleHeight,
    triangleHeight);
18              triangle.graphics.lineTo(0, triangleHeight);
19              triangle.graphics.lineTo(triangleHeight/2, 0);
20
21              this.addChild(triangle);
22          }
23      }
24  }
```

# Shapes

Circles, squares, and rectangles are the most common shapes created with the Drawing API. Fortunately, ActionScript 3 makes creating shapes far easier than AS2 does.

## AS2: Shapes

Circles are more complicated than most of the common shapes that can be created with ActionScript 2. Creating a circle requires custom code and math skills. The following example includes a custom class method called drawCircle to draw a circle base on y, x, radius, and sides values.

Drawing a circle requires a custom class method and some math skills in AS2.

```
 1  class CircleExample extends MovieClip
 2  {
 3
 4      public function CircleExample(Void)
 5      {
 6          this.drawCircle(100, 100, 100, 100);
 7      }
 8
 9      private function drawCircle(centerX:Number, centerY:Number,
    radius:Number, sides:Number):Void
10      {
11          this.lineStyle(10, 0xcccccc, 100, false, "vertical",
    "none", "miter", 10);
12          this.moveTo(centerX + radius,  centerY);
13
14          for(var i:Number=0; i<=sides; i++)
15          {
16              var pointRatio:Number = (i/sides);
17              var xSteps:Number =
    Math.cos(pointRatio*2*Math.PI);
18              var ySteps:Number =
    Math.sin(pointRatio*2*Math.PI);
19              var pointX:Number = (centerX + xSteps * radius);
20              var pointY:Number = (centerY + ySteps * radius);
21              this.lineTo(pointX, pointY);
22          }
23      }
24  }
```

## AS3: Shapes

ActionScript 3 makes creating shapes so much easier than AS2 does. The AS3 way to create a circle, for example, requires much less code and is extremely easy to implement. In AS3 the Graphics object provides methods for drawing common shapes, such as drawRect, drawRoundRect, drawCircle, and drawEllipse.

The following code is an example of the AS3 CircleExample class using the Graphic classes drawCircle method.

```
 1  package
 2  {
 3      import flash.display.Sprite;
 4      import flash.display.LineScaleMode;
 5      import flash.display.CapsStyle;
 6      import flash.display.JointStyle;
 7      import flash.display.Shape;
 8
 9      public class CircleExample extends Sprite
10      {
11          public function CircleExample()
12          {
13              this.graphics.lineStyle(10, 0xcccccc, 1, false,
    LineScaleMode.VERTICAL, CapsStyle.NONE, JointStyle.MITER, 10);
14              this.graphics.drawCircle(100, 100, 100);
15          }
16      }
17  }
```

The Graphics class has a drawCircle method, among many other shape-drawing methods.

# Fills

Fills can be represented by solid colors and gradients with ActionScript. Solid-color fills are pretty straightforward, but gradients, as cool as they are, require a little more thought.

This section shows the differences between AS2 and AS3 in how gradient fills are created, and the improvements that have been made to the functionality in AS3.

## AS2: Fills

Depending on the complexity of the design, gradients can require some planning. This is because of the parameters that a gradient requires. In the GradientExample class, for example, eight variables make up the parameter values for the beginGradientFill method. The variables used are arrays, strings, numbers, and a matrix.

```
1   import flash.geom.*;
2
3   class GradientExample extends MovieClip
4   {
5
6       public function GradientExample(Void)
7       {
8           var colors:Array = [0xcccccc, 0xffffff];
9           var fillType:String = "linear";
10          var alphas:Array = [100, 100];
11          var ratios:Array = [0, 0xFF];
12          var spreadMethod:String = "pad";
13          var interpolationMethod:String = "linearRGB";
14          var focalPointRatio:Number = 0.2;
15          var matrix:Matrix = new Matrix();
16          matrix.createGradientBox(100, 100, 0, 0, 0);
17          beginGradientFill(fillType, colors, alphas, ratios,
    matrix, spreadMethod, interpolationMethod, focalPointRatio);
18          lineTo(0, 100);
19          lineTo(100, 100);
20          lineTo(100, 0);
21          lineTo(0, 0);
22          endFill();
23      }
24  }
```

All of these variables are used to create a gradient and keep the code readable.

beginGradientFill uses the previous variables to create a gradient fill in the graphic that is drawn.

You've probably noticed that there is no movie clip created in order to use the drawing functionality. A movie clip isn't needed in this example because the MovieClip class was inherited; therefore, the GradientExample itself is a movie clip and can utilize the drawing features.

## AS3: Fills

In the ActionScript 3 version of the GradientExample, the code is much more compact and easier to read. First of all, as was mentioned above, the MovieClip class is no longer needed to create graphics. Since the GradientExample inherits the Sprite class, the graphics property is available for drawing. In addition, there are new static classes that define the values used for GradientType and SpreadMethod. These classes eliminate the need to rely on string values that were used in AS2.

```
1   package
2   {
3       import flash.display.*;
4       import flash.geom.*;
5
6       public class GradientExample extends Sprite
7       {
8           public function GradientExample()
9           {
10              var colors:Array = [0xcccccc, 0xffffff];
11              var alphas:Array = [1, 1];
12              var ratios:Array = [0x00, 0xFF];
13              var matr:Matrix = new Matrix();
14              matr.createGradientBox(20, 20, 0, 0, 0);
15              this.graphics.lineStyle(1, 0xcccccc, 1);
16
    this.graphics.beginGradientFill(GradientType.LINEAR, colors,
    alphas, ratios, matr, SpreadMethod.PAD);
17              this.graphics.drawRect(0,0,100,100);
18          }
19      }
20  }
```

> The code to create a gradient fill is easier to read and write with the GradientType and SpreadMethod static classes.

# Color

As far back as ActionScript 1, you could change the color of an item in a Flash movie. The level of control you have in newer versions of ActionScript is much more robust than with the old Color object. The ColorTransform class lets you multiply and offset specific colors rather than simply changing an object from one color to another. The ColorTransform class has been available since AS2, but AS3 has integrated the class into the display architecture, making it much more accessible and easy to implement.

## AS2: Color

Color transforming in ActionScript 2 is not difficult, but it requires a few steps to work. Transforming color starts with the instantiation of the ColorTransform class. Once the class has been instantiated, it needs to be applied with an object called Transform. When instantiated, the Transform class takes the object that you want to apply the color to as a parameter. Then, the instantiated Transform object uses the colorTransform property to apply the new ColorTransform.

```
1   import flash.geom.*;
2
3   class ColorTransformExample extends MovieClip
4   {
5
6       public function ColorTransformExample(Void)
7       {
8           this.drawCircle(100, 100, 100, 100);
9
10          var colorTransform:ColorTransform = new
        ColorTransform(0.5, 1.0, 0.5, 0.5, 10, 10, 10, 0);
11          var trans:Transform = new Transform(this);
12          trans.colorTransform = colorTransform;
13      }
14
15      private function drawCircle(centerX:Number, centerY:Number,
        radius:Number, sides:Number):Void
16      {
17          this.lineStyle(10, 0xcccccc, 100, false, "vertical",
        "none", "miter", 10);
18          this.moveTo(centerX + radius,  centerY);
19
20          for(var i:Number=0; i<=sides; i++)
21          {
22              var pointRatio:Number = (i/sides);
23              var xSteps:Number =
        Math.cos(pointRatio*2*Math.PI);
24              var ySteps:Number =
        Math.sin(pointRatio*2*Math.PI);
25              var pointX:Number = (centerX + xSteps * radius);
26              var pointY:Number = (centerY + ySteps * radius);
27              this.lineTo(pointX, pointY);
28          }
```

ColorTransform and Transform are instantiated and the color transform instance is applied to the transform objects colorTransform property.

```
29        }
30  }
```

The functionality works fine, but it's a little convoluted. ActionScript 3 simplifies the process of drawing a circle into one line of code!

## AS3: Color

Every `DisplayObject` has a property named `transform`. The `transform` property is a `Transform` object that pertains to the display object's matrix, color transform, and pixel bounds. In ActionScript 3, the `transform` property and the `ColorTransform` class must be used together to transform the color of a display object. The `ColorTransformExample` is a clear case of how much cleaner your ActionScript code can be after utilizing all the techniques learned in this chapter. For example, you no longer need to create a movie clip to draw, you don't need a custom method to create a circle, all string values have been replaced by static classes, and all display objects include `graphics` and `transform` properties that provide complete drawing and color transforming capabilities.

`ColorTransform` must be imported for use in the class.

Since the class is a `DisplayObject`, it includes a `transform` property to use the `colorTransform`.

```
1   package
2   {
3       import flash.display.*;
4       import flash.geom.ColorTransform;
5
6       public class ColorTransformExample extends Sprite
7       {
8           public function ColorTransformExample()
9           {
10              this.graphics.lineStyle(10, 0xcccccc, 1, false,
    LineScaleMode.VERTICAL, CapsStyle.NONE, JointStyle.MITER, 10);
11              this.graphics.drawCircle(100, 100, 100);
12              this.transform.colorTransform =
    new ColorTransform(1, 1, 1, 1, 25, 0, 25, 0);
13          }
14      }
15  }
```

CHAPTER 12

# Animation

FLASH AND ANIMATION are almost synonymous. Although ActionScript gives Flash abilities that go far beyond simple animation, animators are still a key part of the audience for Flash. The software is used to create commercials, videos, and even television shows—such as Cartoon Network's Emmy-Award-winning *Foster's Home for Imaginary Friends*. AS2 brought animation to a new level with the undocumented Tween object, and things have only gotten better in AS3. This chapter covers the differences when creating Tween object instances and handling tween events in AS2 and AS3, and introduces the improvements in AS3.

# Tweening

Scaling, fading in and out, rotating, or any simple animation can be accomplished with the Tween object. The functionality is essentially the same, but the ActionScript packages have been updated and the Tween object is officially documented in Flash help. This section takes a look at these updates.

## AS2: Tweening

The following code is an example that builds on code in the previous chapter. The custom drawCircle method creates a MovieClip, then the Tween object animates the circle horizontally across the stage. The Tween object creates an animation based on seven parameters: the item being animated; the property that you want to effect, such as the _x or _y axis; the easing method; start position; end position; time; and finally, a Boolean to determine whether to use seconds or the timeline as the timing mechanism.

Tween animates the circle movie clip horizontally across the stage over three frames.

```
1   import mx.utils.Delegate;
2   import mx.transitions.Tween;
3   import mx.transitions.easing.*;
4
5   class TweenExample extends MovieClip
6   {
7       public function TweenExample(Void)
8       {
9           var circle:MovieClip =
    this.drawCircle(25, 25, 25, 25);
10          var myTween:Tween = new Tween(circle, "_x",
    Elastic.easeOut, 0, (Stage.width-circle._width), 3, true);
11      }
12
13      private function drawCircle(centerX:Number, centerY:Number,
    radius:Number, sides:Number):MovieClip
14      {
15          var circle:MovieClip =
    MovieClip(this.createEmptyMovieClip("circle",
    this.getNextHighestDepth()));
16          circle.lineStyle(2, 0xcccccc, 100, false, "vertical",
    "none", "miter", 10);
17          circle.moveTo(centerX + radius,  centerY);
18
19          for(var i:Number=0; i<=sides; i++)
20          {
```

```
21              var pointRatio:Number = (i/sides);
22              var xSteps:Number =
Math.cos(pointRatio*2*Math.PI);
23              var ySteps:Number =
Math.sin(pointRatio*2*Math.PI);
24            var pointX:Number = (centerX + xSteps * radius);
25            var pointY:Number = (centerY + ySteps * radius);
26            circle.lineTo(pointX, pointY);
27        }
28
29        return circle;
30      }
31  }
```

## AS3: Tweening

As mentioned earlier, the Tween object is essentially the same in ActionScript 3, but now it is officially documented and the class paths have been updated. Another difference is some of the properties that you will use as parameters—such as x, y, xscale, yscale, and rotation—no longer use the underscore.

The Tween class and easing package have been relocated to the fl.transitions package.

Tween takes the circle sprite and animates it horizontally across the stage by targeting the x property.

```
1   package
2   {
3       import flash.display.*;
4       import fl.transitions.Tween;
5       import fl.transitions.easing.*;
6
7       public class TweenExample extends Sprite
8       {
9
10          public function TweenExample()
11          {
12              var circle:Sprite = new Sprite();
13              circle.graphics.beginFill(0xcccccc);
14              circle.graphics.drawCircle(25, 25, 25);
15              addChild(circle);
16
17              var circleTween:Tween = new Tween(circle, "x",
Elastic.easeOut, 0, stage.width, 3, true);
18          }
19
20      }
21  }
```

# Events

Events drive what occurs in a Flash movie, and the Tween object is no exception to the new event-handling model. The old callback-function properties from the Tween class in ActionScript 2 have been updated to a new event object that is designed for the Tween class in AS3.

## AS2: Events

Event handling is the life force in Flash, and the Tween object has five events that can trigger custom functionality—start, stop, resume, finish, and even a change in the Tween object. The TweenExample shows how two different callback-function properties from the Tween object can fire custom class methods when they occur.

```
1   import mx.utils.Delegate;
2   import mx.transitions.Tween;
3   import mx.transitions.easing.*;
4
5   class TweenExample extends MovieClip
6   {
7       public function TweenExample(Void)
8       {
9           var circle:MovieClip = this.drawCircle(25, 25, 25,
    25);
10          var myTween:Tween = new Tween(circle, "_x",
    Elastic.easeOut, 0, (Stage.width-circle._width), 3, true);
11          myTween.onMotionChanged =
    Delegate.create(this, onMotionChanged);
12          myTween.onMotionFinished =
    Delegate.create(this, onMotionFinished);
13      }
14
15      private function onMotionChanged(Void):Void
16      {
17          trace("onMotionChanged");
18      }
19
20      private function onMotionFinished(Void):Void
21      {
22          trace("onMotionFinished");
23      }
```

onMotionChanged and onMotionFinished are two of five callback-function properties. When used in a class, they can be delegated to a custom class method.

```
24
25      private function drawCircle(centerX:Number, centerY:Number,
    radius:Number, sides:Number):MovieClip
26      {
27          var circle:MovieClip =
    MovieClip(this.createEmptyMovieClip("circle",
    this.getNextHighestDepth()));
28          circle.lineStyle(2, 0xcccccc, 100, false, "vertical",
    "none", "miter", 10);
29          circle.moveTo(centerX + radius,  centerY);
30
31          for(var i:Number=0; i<=sides; i++)
32          {
33              var pointRatio:Number = (i/sides);
34              var xSteps:Number =
    (Math.cos(pointRatio*2*Math.PI));
35              var ySteps:Number =
    Math.sin(pointRatio*2*Math.PI);
36              var pointX:Number = (centerX + xSteps * radius);
37              var pointY:Number = (centerY + ySteps * radius);
38              circle.lineTo(pointX, pointY);
39          }
40
41          return circle;
42      }
43  }
```

## AS3: Events

ActionScript 3 takes a more orderly approach to events with the new
TweenEvent class. The TweenEvent class contains static properties that
represent the events that can occur with a Tween object instance. The same
events are available with the updated Tween class, but are now stored in the
handy TweenEvent class.

The next example shows how listeners are added to a Tween instance in
order to dispatch an event when the animation has changed or finished.
When an event is fired from the TweenEvent class, it can easily call a custom
class method. The method receives a parameter value that is a TweenEvent
and provides details about the event when it occurs.

TweenEvent is a new class that is imported to dispatch events from the Tween object.

Tween instances can listen to different events in the TweenEvent class.

Custom methods can be called when a TweenEvent fires. The TweenEvent is passed as a parameter value to provide details about the event.

```
1   package
2   {
3       import flash.display.*;
4       import fl.transitions.Tween;
5       import fl.transitions.easing.*;
6       import fl.transitions.TweenEvent;
7
8       public class TweenExample extends Sprite
9       {
10
11          public function TweenExample()
12          {
13              var circle:Sprite = new Sprite();
14              circle.graphics.beginFill(0xcccccc);
15              circle.graphics.drawCircle(25, 25, 25);
16              addChild(circle);
17
18              var circleTween:Tween = new Tween(circle, "x",
    Elastic.easeOut, 0, stage.width, 3, true);
19
    circleTween.addEventListener(TweenEvent.MOTION_CHANGE,
    this.onMotionChanged);
20
    circleTween.addEventListener(TweenEvent.MOTION_FINISH,
    this.onMotionComplete);
21          }
22
23          private function
    onMotionChanged(event:TweenEvent):void
24          {
25              trace("onMotionChanged: "+ event);
26          }
27
28          private function
    onMotionComplete(event:TweenEvent):void
29          {
30              trace("onMotionComplete: "+ event);
31          }
32
33      }
34  }
```

# CHAPTER 13

# Sound

LET'S FACE IT—SOUND IS FUN to work with! Unfortunately, when working with sound in ActionScript 2, we've had to create a lot of the functionality ourselves, using custom code. In ActionScript 3, we no longer need to write custom code when working with the Sound object, but in general, we have to write more lines to achieve the same effects. Fortunately, existing code is always easier to write than customized code.

# Loading

The ability to play sound with ActionScript usually begins with the loading of an external MP3.

## AS2: Loading

Loading an external sound file with ActionScript 2 is fairly simple. First you create a Sound object instance and add it as a class property for later access in the class. Once the Sound instance is created, the loadSound function loads an MP3. The onLoad callback-function property tells the script when the loading is complete and the sound is ready to play, and the start function is used to start the sound.

```
1   import mx.utils.Delegate;
2
3   class SoundExample extends MovieClip
4   {
5       private var sound:Sound;
6
7       public function SoundExample(Void)
8       {
9           this.sound = new Sound();
10          this.sound.loadSound("path/file.mp3", true);
11          this.sound.onLoad = Delegate.create(this,
    onSoundLoaded);
12      }
13
14      private function onSoundLoaded(Void):Void
15      {
16          this.sound.start(0);
17      }
18  }
```

A sound property is added for full class access.

A Sound object is instantiated, an MP3 file is loaded, and the onLoad event is assigned to a custom class method.

SoundLoaded is triggered when the onLoad event occurs and activates the start function.

## AS3: Loading

With ActionScript 3, external sound files need to be loaded like any other external file, in the form of a URLRequest. The URLRequest is instantiated with the path to an external MP3 file and loaded via the sound object's load function. Once loaded, the play function, rather than the start function, is used to begin the audio.

```
1   package
2   {
3       import flash.display.Sprite;
4       import flash.net.URLRequest;
5       import flash.media.Sound;
6
7       public class SoundExample extends Sprite
8       {
9           public function SoundExample()
10          {
11              var uRequest:URLRequest =
    new URLRequest("path/file.mp3");
12              var sound:Sound = new Sound();
13              sound.load(uRequest);
14              sound.play();
15          }
16
17      }
18  }
```

The URLRequest and Sound classes are imported to request a file and create a Sound object.

URLRequest is instantiated with the path to an external MP3 file.

load takes a URLRequest instead of a string path.

play is the new start for Sound objects.

# Events

There are numerous events associated with the Sound object in ActionScript. One important event that is missing in AS2 is a way to track progress. This section shows how to track progress with a custom method in AS2 versus how to track progress with AS3.

## AS2: Events

In ActionScript 2, the Sound class provides functions that let you determine the bytes loaded and the total bytes of an external sound file while it is loading, but does not offer an event to help track progress. Therefore, you have to write custom code to handle tracking progress.

Progress must be determined by continuously checking the loaded bytes and total bytes. There are a number of ways to execute code continuously. In the following example, the onEnterFrame function is used to call a custom method named onSoundProgress repeatedly until the sound file has finished loading. While the onSoundProgress method is being executed, progress can be determined by calculating the loaded bytes versus the total bytes.

```
1   import mx.utils.Delegate;
2
3   class SoundExample extends MovieClip
4   {
5       private var sound:Sound;
6
7       public function SoundExample(Void)
8       {
9           this.sound = new Sound();
10          this.sound.loadSound("path/file.mp3", true);
11          this.onEnterFrame = Delegate.create(this,
    onSoundProgress);
12          this.sound.onLoad = Delegate.create(this,
    onSoundLoaded);
13          this.sound.onSoundComplete = Delegate.create(this,
    onSoundComplete);
14      }
15
16      private function onSoundProgress(Void):Void
17      {
18          trace("Loaded: "+ this.sound.getBytesLoaded() +",
    Total: "+ this.sound.getBytesTotal());
19      }
20
21      private function onSoundLoaded(Void):Void
22      {
23          this.onEnterFrame = null;
24          this.sound.start(0);
25      }
26
27      private function onSoundComplete(Void):Void
28      {
29          trace("onSoundComplete");
30      }
31
32  }
```

onEnterFrame repeatedly executes a custom class method to track loading progress.

The getBytesLoaded and getBytesTotal functions are used to track progress.

Once the file is loaded, the onEnterFrame function is set to null to stop it from executing.

While this example works, it's more of a quick fix for an event that is missing from the ActionScript language.

## AS3: Events

ActionScript 3 handles measuring progress universally, using the same tools regardless of the class. When a file is requested, the ProgressEvent class can be added as a listener, and its PROGRESS property can be used to continuously execute a custom class method. Rather than relying on the onEnterFrame event, the code is built in and condensed to one line of code.

During the loading progress, you can determine the number of bytes that have been loaded and the total number of bytes via two properties of the ProgressEvent parameter value. These properties—bytesLoaded and bytesTotal—replace AS2's getBytesLoaded and getBytesTotal functions.

The events package is imported to track progress.

ProgressEvent.PROGRESS executes a class method during the loading progress.

ProgressEvent is used to track loading through the bytesLoaded and bytesTotal properties. No custom code is needed.

```
1  package
2  {
3      import flash.display.Sprite;
4      import flash.net.URLRequest;
5      import flash.events.*;
6      import flash.media.Sound;
7
8      public class SoundExample extends Sprite
9      {
10
11         public function SoundExample()
12         {
13             var uRequest:URLRequest =
   new URLRequest("path/file.mp3");
14             var sound:Sound = new Sound();
15             sound.addEventListener(ProgressEvent.PROGRESS,
   this.onSoundLoading);
16             sound.addEventListener(Event.COMPLETE,
   this.onSoundLoaded);
17             sound.load(uRequest);
18             sound.play();
19         }
20
21         private function
   onSoundLoading(event:ProgressEvent):void
22         {
23             trace("Loaded: "+ event.bytesLoaded, "Total: "+
   event.bytesTotal);
24         }
25
```

```
26        private function onSoundLoaded(event:Event):void
27        {
28            trace("onSoundLoaded: "+ event);
29        }
30
31    }
32 }
```

# Volume

Setting the volume is extremely easy with ActionScript 2, as it only calls for a single line of code. In AS3, volume is a little more complicated, but you also have more control. In this section, you will see the differences between the two versions in how to control volume with a dynamic volume controller.

## AS2: Volume

When ActionScript 2 is simpler than ActionScript 3, it's usually because there is not as much control over the resulting functionality. Volume is an example of a simpler approach to functionality, as AS2 only requires a single line of code. We use the Sound class's setVolume function, which takes 0–100 as a parameter for the sound level.

In the following SoundExample class, a controller is created using the drawCircle method (see Chapter 12), with press and release actions that trigger dragging functionality. While the dragging occurs, the volume is set based on the x-axis of the circle movie clip, which is restricted to move from 0 to 100.

```
1  import mx.utils.Delegate;
2
3  class SoundExample extends MovieClip
4  {
5      private var sound:Sound;
6      private var circle:MovieClip;
7
8      public function SoundExample(Void)
9      {
10         this.sound = new Sound();
11         this.sound.loadSound("path/file.mp3", true);
12         this.onEnterFrame =
   Delegate.create(this, onSoundProgress);
```

circle is added as a property for total class access.

| | |
|---|---|
| | ```
13        this.sound.onLoad =
    Delegate.create(this, onSoundLoaded);
14            this.sound.onSoundComplete =
    Delegate.create(this, onSoundComplete);
15
``` |

**drawCircle** creates a circle as a volume control, and actions are applied to initiate drag functionality.

```
16            this.circle = this.drawCircle(25, 25, 25, 100);
17            this.circle.useHandCursor = true;
18            this.circle.onPress =
    Delegate.create(this, startDragItem);
19            this.circle.onRelease = this.circle.onReleaseOutside
    = Delegate.create(this, stopDragItem);
20
```

The circle and volume are both set to 50.

```
21            this.circle._x = 50;
22            this.circle.setVolume(this.circle._x);
23        }
24
```

**startDragItem** creates a recurring call to **onDragItem** and creates drag functionality.

```
25        private function startDragItem(Void):Void
26        {
27            this.circle.onEnterFrame =
    Delegate.create(this, onDragItem);
28            this.circle.startDrag(true, 0, 0, 100, 0);
29        }
30
```

**onDragItem** sets the volume based on the x-axis of the **circle**, which can be moved from 0 to 100.

```
31        private function onDragItem(Void):Void
32        {
33            this.sound.setVolume(this.circle._x);
34        }
35
```

When the **circle** is released, **stopDragItem** stops onEnterFrame and the drag functionality.

```
36        private function stopDragItem(Void):Void
37        {
38            this.circle.onEnterFrame = null;
39            this.circle.stopDrag();
40        }
41
42        private function onSoundProgress(Void):Void
43        {
44            trace("Loaded: "+ this.sound.getBytesLoaded() +",
    Total: "+ this.sound.getBytesTotal());
45        }
46
47        private function onSoundLoaded(Void):Void
48        {
```
```

```
49              this.onEnterFrame = null;
50              this.sound.start(0);
51          }
52
53      private function onSoundComplete(Void):Void
54      {
55          trace("onSoundComplete");
56      }
57
58      private function drawCircle(centerX:Number, centerY:Number,
    radius:Number, sides:Number):MovieClip
59      {
60          var _circle:MovieClip =
    MovieClip(this.createEmptyMovieClip("circle", 1));
61          _circle.beginFill(0xcccccc, 100)
62          _circle.moveTo(centerX + radius,  centerY);
63
64          for(var i:Number=0; i<=sides; i++)
65          {
66              var pointRatio:Number = (i/sides);
67              var xSteps:Number =
    Math.cos(pointRatio*2*Math.PI);
68              var ySteps:Number =
    Math.sin(pointRatio*2*Math.PI);
69              var pointX:Number = (centerX + xSteps * radius);
70              var pointY:Number = (centerY + ySteps * radius);
71              _circle.lineTo(pointX, pointY);
72          }
73          return _circle;
74      }
75
76  }
```

> drawCircle is used to create a volume control.

## AS3: Volume

In ActionScript 3, volume control is more than a global volume for all sounds in a Flash movie. Volume is now based on channels and is controlled through the soundTransform property of the SoundChannel class. The soundTransform property is a SoundTransform object instance assigned to the SoundChannel class and is used to control panning, speaker assignment, and volume. In AS3 every sound has a sound channel, and a Flash movie can have multiple sound channels, which can be used to create sophisticated sound applications.

The following SoundExample class uses the same functionality as the previous AS2 SoundExample does, but utilizes the new Sound, SoundChannel, and SoundTransform classes. You'll notice that this example has one channel, which is assigned to the sound instance when it begins to play. This channel property is then used to control the volume via a SoundTransform object while the volume control is dragged. Like other numerical values in AS3, the sound volume now takes a number between 0 and 1, where 0=0 and 1=100.

SoundChannel and SoundTransform are imported to control sound volume.

The Rectangle class is imported to define dragging bounds.

channel is scoped as a property for access throughout the class.

channel is assigned to the currently playing sound.

A circle is created as a volume control.

The buttonMode and useHandCursor properties are set to true to show the hand cursor when rolling over the circle.

```
1    package
2    {
3        import flash.display.Sprite;
4        import flash.net.URLRequest;
5        import flash.events.*;
6        import flash.media.Sound;
7        import flash.media.SoundChannel;
8        import flash.media.SoundTransform;
9        import flash.geom.Rectangle;
10
11       public class SoundExample extends Sprite
12       {
13           private var channel:SoundChannel;
14           private var circle:Sprite;
15
16           public function SoundExample()
17           {
18               var uRequest:URLRequest =
     new URLRequest("path/file.mp3");
19               var sound:Sound = new Sound();
20               sound.addEventListener(ProgressEvent.PROGRESS,
     this.onSoundLoading);
21               sound.addEventListener(Event.COMPLETE,
     this.onSoundLoaded);
22               sound.load(uRequest);
23               this.channel = sound.play();
24
25               this.circle = new Sprite();
26               this.circle.graphics.beginFill(0xcccccc);
27               this.circle.graphics.drawCircle(25, 25, 25);
28               addChild(this.circle);
29               this.circle.buttonMode = true;
30               this.circle.useHandCursor = true;
```

The MOUSE_DOWN event is used to execute dragging.

```
                    this.circle.addEventListener(
MouseEvent.MOUSE_DOWN, this.startDragItem);

                    this.circle.x = 50;
                    this.setVolume(this.circle.x/100);
            }
```

setVolume sets the volume based on a number value.

X-axis bounds are set to 0–100 via the Rectangle class. MOUSE_UP and MOUSE_MOVE events are added to the stage to determine release and movement of the circle.

```
        private function startDragItem(event:MouseEvent):void
        {
                    this.circle.startDrag(true,
new Rectangle(0, 0, 100, 0));
                    stage.addEventListener(MouseEvent.MOUSE_UP,
stopDragItem);
                    stage.addEventListener(MouseEvent.MOUSE_MOVE,
onDragItem);
            }
```

The MOUSE_MOVE event from startDragItem executes onDragItem, which sets volume based on the x-axis of the circle.

```
        private function onDragItem(event:MouseEvent):void
        {
                    this.setVolume(this.circle.x/100);
            }
```

stopDragItem executes when the circle is released. MOUSE_UP and MOUSE_MOVE are removed and the dragging stops.

```
        private function stopDragItem(event:MouseEvent):void
        {
                    stage.removeEventListener(MouseEvent.MOUSE_UP,
stopDragItem);
                    stage.removeEventListener(MouseEvent.MOUSE_MOVE,
onDragItem);
                    this.circle.stopDrag();
            }
```

SoundTransform is instantiated to assign a volume level. Then transform is assigned to the soundTransform property of the channel.

```
        private function setVolume(_volume:Number):void
        {
                    var transform:SoundTransform =
this.channel.soundTransform;
                    transform.volume = _volume;
                    this.channel.soundTransform = transform;
            }

        private function onSoundLoading(event:ProgressEvent):
void
            {
```

Line numbers: 31 32 33 34 35 36 37 38 39 40 41 42 43 44 45 46 47 48 49 50 51 52 53 54 55 56 57 58 59 60 61 62 63 64

```
65          trace("Loaded: "+ event.bytesLoaded, "Total: "+
     event.bytesTotal);
66          }
67
68          private function onSoundLoaded(event:Event):void
69          {
70              trace("onSoundLoaded: "+ event);
71          }
72
73      }
74  }
```

# ID3 Tags

ID3 metadata contains information about an MP3 file, such as the album name and artist, comment, genre, song name, track number, year of recording, and so on. ActionScript is capable of retrieving the ID3 data through the Sound class.

## AS2: ID3 Tags

ID3 tags are available through the Sound class's id3 property. When loading external MP3 files, as in the previous SoundExample, ID3 metadata is not available immediately. The onID3 callback-function property must be used to determine when ID3 data is available and can be accessed.

The id3 property has a number of properties of its own that are pretty easy to remember. The following example accesses the artist and songname properties of the id3 tag after the onID3 event executes.

```
1  import mx.utils.Delegate;
2
3  class SoundExample extends MovieClip
4  {
5      private var sound:Sound;
6      private var circle:MovieClip;
7
8      public function SoundExample(Void)
9      {
10         this.sound = new Sound();
11         this.sound.loadSound("path/file.mp3", true);
```

The onID3 callback-function property executes a custom class method when the ID3 information is available to ActionScript.

```
12          this.onEnterFrame =
     Delegate.create(this, onSoundProgress);
13          this.sound.onLoad =
     Delegate.create(this, onSoundLoaded);
14          this.sound.onSoundComplete =
     Delegate.create(this, onSoundComplete);
15          this.sound.onID3 = Delegate.create(this, onID3);
16
17          this.circle = this.drawCircle(25, 25, 25, 100);
18          this.circle.useHandCursor = true;
19          this.circle.onPress =
     Delegate.create(this, startDragItem);
20          this.circle.onRelease = this.circle.onReleaseOutside
     = Delegate.create(this, stopDragItem);
21
22          this.circle._x = 50;
23          this.circle.setVolume(this.circle._x);
24      }
25
26      private function startDragItem(Void):Void
27      {
28          this.circle.onEnterFrame =
     Delegate.create(this, onDragItem);
29          this.circle.startDrag(true, 0, 0, 100, 0);
30      }
31
32      private function onDragItem(Void):Void
33      {
34          this.sound.setVolume(this.circle._x);
35      }
36
37      private function stopDragItem(Void):Void
38      {
39          this.circle.onEnterFrame = null;
40          this.circle.stopDrag();
41      }
42
43      private function onSoundProgress(Void):Void
44      {
45          trace("Loaded: "+ this.sound.getBytesLoaded() +",
     Total: "+ this.sound.getBytesTotal());
46      }
47
```

onID3 executes when ID3 info is available. The sound instance can then access the id3 property and id3 values, such as artist and songname.

```
48        private function onSoundLoaded(Void):Void
49        {
50            this.onEnterFrame = null;
51            this.sound.start(0);
52        }
53
54        private function onID3(Void):Void
55        {
56            if(this.sound.id3.artist) trace("Artist: "+ this.
sound.id3.artist);
57            if(this.sound.id3.songname) trace("Song Name: "+
this.sound.id3.songname);
58        }
59
60        private function onSoundComplete(Void):Void
61        {
62            trace("onSoundComplete");
63        }
64
65        private function drawCircle(centerX:Number, centerY:Number,
radius:Number, sides:Number):MovieClip
66        {
67            var _circle:MovieClip =
MovieClip(this.createEmptyMovieClip("circle", 1));
68            _circle.beginFill(0xcccccc, 100)
69            _circle.moveTo(centerX + radius,  centerY);
70
71            for(var i:Number=0; i<=sides; i++)
72            {
73                var pointRatio:Number = (i/sides);
74                var xSteps:Number =
Math.cos(pointRatio*2*Math.PI);
75                var ySteps:Number =
Math.sin(pointRatio*2*Math.PI);
76                var pointX:Number = (centerX + xSteps * radius);
77                var pointY:Number = (centerY + ySteps * radius);
78                _circle.lineTo(pointX, pointY);
79            }
80            return _circle;
81        }
82
83  }
```

## AS3: ID3 Tags

ID3 tags are also accessible in ActionScript 3. In fact, an entire class named ID3Info is dedicated to them. The Sound class has the same id3 property as in ActionScript 2, but the property is now an instance of the ID3Info class. The ID3Info class contains all the properties that were available in AS2, some of which are not actually defined as class properties.

Just as in AS2, the ID3 values cannot be accessed until an event occurs; in AS3, this event is Event.ID3. A sound instance can add an event listener and execute a custom class method when ID3 info is available. The custom class method in the code below, named onID3Available, accesses two of the ID3Info properties: artist and songName.

```
1   package
2   {
3       import flash.display.Sprite;
4       import flash.net.URLRequest;
5       import flash.events.*;
6       import flash.media.Sound;
7       import flash.media.SoundChannel;
8       import flash.media.SoundTransform;
9       import flash.geom.Rectangle;
10
11      public class SoundExample extends Sprite
12      {
13          private var channel:SoundChannel;
14          private var circle:Sprite;
15
16          public function SoundExample()
17          {
18              var uRequest:URLRequest = new
    URLRequest("path/file.mp3");
19              var sound:Sound = new Sound();
20              sound.addEventListener(ProgressEvent.PROGRESS,
    this.onSoundLoading);
21              sound.addEventListener(Event.COMPLETE,
    this.onSoundLoaded);
22              sound.addEventListener(Event.ID3,
    this.onID3Available);
23              sound.load(uRequest);
24              this.channel = sound.play();
25
26
```

The Event object contains an ID3 event to execute a class method when the id3 information is available for a loaded file.

```
27              this.circle = new Sprite();
28              this.circle.graphics.beginFill(0xcccccc);
29              this.circle.graphics.drawCircle(25, 25, 25);
30              addChild(this.circle);
31              this.circle.buttonMode = true;
32              this.circle.useHandCursor = true;
33              this.circle.addEventListener(
    MouseEvent.MOUSE_DOWN, this.startDragItem);
34
35              this.circle.x = 50;
36              this.setVolume(this.circle.x/100);
37          }
38
39          private function startDragItem(event:MouseEvent):void
40          {
41              this.circle.startDrag(true, new Rectangle(0, 0,
    100, 0));
42              stage.addEventListener(MouseEvent.MOUSE_UP,
    stopDragItem);
43              stage.addEventListener(MouseEvent.MOUSE_MOVE,
    onDragItem);
44          }
45
46          private function onDragItem(event:MouseEvent):void
47          {
48              this.setVolume(this.circle.x/100);
49          }
50
51          private function stopDragItem(event:MouseEvent):void
52          {
53              stage.removeEventListener(MouseEvent.MOUSE_UP,
    stopDragItem);
54              stage.removeEventListener(MouseEvent.MOUSE_MOVE,
    onDragItem);
55              this.circle.stopDrag();
56          }
57
58          private function setVolume(_volume:Number):void
59          {
60              var transform:SoundTransform =
    this.channel.soundTransform;
61              transform.volume = _volume;
```

```
62              this.channel.soundTransform = transform;
63          }
64
65          private function onSoundLoading(event:ProgressEvent):
    void
66          {
67              trace("Loaded: "+ event.bytesLoaded, "Total: "+
    event.bytesTotal);
68          }
69
70          private function onSoundLoaded(event:Event):void
71          {
72              trace("onSoundLoaded: "+ event);
73          }
74
75          private function onID3Available(event:Event):void
76          {
77              trace("onID3Available: "+ event);
78              var sound:Sound = Sound(event.currentTarget);
79              if(sound.id3.artist) trace("Artist: "+
    sound.id3.artist);
80              if(sound.id3.songName) trace("Song Name: "+
    sound.id3.songName);
81          }
82      }
83  }
```

onID3Available is executed as the custom class method when the id3 information is available to the sound object instance.

CHAPTER 14

# More Reasons to
# Make the Switch

IN ADDITION TO THE major overhaul in the structure and architecture of the language, ActionScript 3 introduced some exciting new features that make ActionScript development much more powerful. This chapter covers completely new features that are built into the language, including event bubbling, label statements, namespaces, and animating with external XML.

If there were not already enough reasons in this book to make the switch, this chapter should be pretty convincing.

# Event Bubbling

As covered earlier, the event-handling architecture in AS3 is a far cry from AS2's. But there's more: event bubbling is built into the event architecture, making it easier than ever to dispatch an event from a DisplayObject. You can subsequently call every ancestor of that DisplayObject, which keeps every layer in a particular display list informed.

In addition to the bubbling from the current DisplayObject through the ancestor tree, addEventListener has an optional third parameter named useCapture. In the following BubblingExample, when useCapture is set to true, the event executes from the stage, to root, to rect. When useCapture is set to false or left empty, the events execute as usual, from the rect, to root, to stage.

Better yet, you can use either option by adding two listeners to the stage and root, one with useCapture set to false or empty, and the other with useCapture set to true. With two event listeners, the event goes up from the stage, to root, to rect, and back down to root and then stage. This is where the difference between the target and currentTarget property becomes apparent. The target property is set to the DisplayObject that originally dispatched the event—in this case rect—while the currentTarget property is set to the DisplayObject in which the event is currently executing. In the following example, currentTarget returns rect, root, and stage as the event bubbles to each object.

```
1   package
2   {
3       import flash.display.*;
4       import flash.events.*;
5
6       public class BubblingExample extends Sprite
7       {
8           public function BubblingExample()
9           {
10              var rect:Sprite = new Sprite();
11              rect.graphics.clear();
12              rect.graphics.beginFill(0x000000);
13              rect.graphics.drawRect(0, 0, 200, 100);
14              addChild(rect);
15
```

> Listeners are added to rect, root, and stage for mouse clicks. The stage and root have one additional listener with a third parameter value set to true for useCapture.

```
16      rect.addEventListener(MouseEvent.CLICK,
onRectangleClicked);
17          root.addEventListener(MouseEvent.CLICK,
onRootClicked);
18          root.addEventListener(MouseEvent.CLICK,
onRootClicked, true);
19          stage.addEventListener(MouseEvent.CLICK,
onStageClicked);
20          stage.addEventListener(MouseEvent.CLICK,
onStageClicked, true);
21      }
22
23      private function onRectangleClicked(event:MouseEvent)
:void
24      {
25          trace("rectangle: "+ event.currentTarget,
event.target);
26      }
27
28      private function onRootClicked(event:MouseEvent):void
29      {
30          trace("root: "+ event.currentTarget,
event.target);
31      }
32
33      private function onStageClicked(event:MouseEvent):void
34      {
35          trace("stage: "+ event.currentTarget,
event.target);
36      }
37   }
38 }
```

> When rect is clicked, onRectangleClicked, onRootClicked, and onStageClicked methods all execute. The target always points to the rect property, while the currentTarget points to the DisplayObject that the method corresponds to in the listeners identified above.

If you would like to stop the propagation of events at a certain point, you can use the stopPropagation function of the event object. For example, if you want to stop the propagation of events when the click event occurs on the root, you could use the following code in the onRootClicked method from the previous example.

```
1 private function onRootClicked(event:MouseEvent):void
2 {
3     trace("root: "+ event.currentTarget, event.target);
4     event.stopPropagation();
5 }
```

# Label Statements

Labels are one of my favorite new features in ActionScript 3. If you have ever used a loop to iterate an array and find a specific value, then you know that by default the loop continues processing until it has completed. There are ways around this in ActionScript 2, such as setting the index to the final number used in the loop, or returning the specific value you are looking for if the loop is run in a function that is returning the specific value. These solutions work fine but need to be completely customized depending on the situation.

AS3 provides label statements, which you can assign to your loop sort of like you do with a variable; but instead of using the equals sign, you use the label, followed by a colon and then the loop you are assigning the label to. The benefit of the label statement is that you can access the label by name at any point and have it stop the loop whenever you please by using the break statement, followed by the label. Imagine that you have a large array of animals and need to get the index of a particular animal in the array. Iterating thousands of records could be slow, but a label statement could reduce the memory consumption by breaking the loop when the animal is found, as in the following example.

An array is defined, and a custom getIndexFromArrayValue method finds the index where the cheetah is located in the array.

Since an array can contain any value type, the wildcard is used for the _value parameter type.

```
1   package
2   {
3       import flash.display.*;
4
5       public class LabelExample extends Sprite
6       {
7           public function LabelExample()
8           {
9               var animals:Array = new Array("giraffe", "lion",
    "cheetah", "polar bear", "monkey");
10              var index:Number =
    this.getIndexFromArrayValue(animals, "cheetah");
11              trace("Index of cheetah: "+ index);
12          }
13
14          private function getIndexFromArrayValue(arr:Array,
    _value:*):Number
15          {
```

| | |
|---|---|
| myLoop is used as a label for the loop. The loop iterates the arr searching for the _value. When the _value is found in arr, the index is set as a return value and the break myLoop statement stops the loop from further iterations. | 16 17 18 19 20 21 22 23 24 25 26 27 28 29 |

```
var index:Number;
myLoop: for(var i:int=0; i<arr.length; i++)
{
    if(arr[i] == _value)
    {
        index = i;
        break myLoop;
    }
    trace(i);
}
return index;
        }
    }
}
```

# Namespace Definition Keyword

Another one of my favorite features is the namespace definition keyword. A namespace eliminates the need to create a separate class for associative arrays, or even to separate classes when it makes more sense to keep logic in one class. For example, if you had to create a class for employees in a company and each employee had slight differences in his or her job description, the namespace keyword would be a great way to differentiate this information. The following Employee class uses two namespaces to differentiate a Designer and a Developer. The Designer and Developer namespaces then define some of the skills for those specific job functions. And finally, a Namespace property named ns differentiates which employee namespace is currently in use.

| | |
|---|---|
| | 1 2 3 4 |
| Designer and Developer namespaces are defined for the Employee class. | 5 6 7 8 |
| Designer and Developer namespaces define skills. | 9 |
| ns property defines the namespace currently used in the class. | 10 11 12 |

```
package
{
    import flash.display.*;

    public class Employee extends Sprite
    {
        private namespace Designer;
        private namespace Developer;
        Designer var skills:String = "Flash, Adobe Photoshop,
Adobe Illustrator";
        Developer var skills:String = "ActionScript";
        private var ns:Namespace;
```

When an Employee is instantiated, the str value related to the job title determines which namespace the employee pertains to.

```actionscript
13      public function Employee(str:String)
14      {
15          switch(str)
16          {
17              case "designer":
18                  ns = Designer;
19                  break;
20              case "developer":
21                  ns = Developer;
22                  break;
23              default:
24          }
25      }
26
27      public function GetSkills():String
28      {
29          return ns::skills;
30      }
31  }
32 }
```

GetSkills returns the skills for the employee based on the current namespace.

The NamespaceExample shows how the Employee class can be used to differentiate the employee type in the Employee constructor. The appropriate namespace is assigned to the Employee instance, and the correct skills for that employee are returned.

```actionscript
1  package
2  {
3      import flash.display.*;
4
5      public class NamespaceExample extends Sprite
6      {
7          public function NamespaceExample()
8          {
9              var developer:Employee =
   new Employee("developer");
10             trace("Developer skills: "+
   developer.GetSkills());
11
12             var designer:Employee = new Employee("designer");
13             trace("Designer skills: "+ designer.GetSkills());
14         }
15     }
16 }
```

A developer Employee is instantiated, and the skills from the Developer namespace are returned from the GetSkills method.

A designer Employee is instantiated, and the skills from the Designer namespace are returned from the GetSkills method.

# Motion XML and the Animator

The Flash AS3 Components API offers some powerful animation features, which are not part of the core ActionScript 3 Flash API. This API includes a new class named Animator. The Animator class bases the animations it creates on XML—or, specifically, Motion XML. Motion XML can be defined in an external XML file, as in the following example, which defines the animation that the Animator class will use in the AnimatorExample class below.

The XML file defines a simple animation that will rotate a DisplayObject across the screen clockwise with a slight ease.

The rotateDirection and rotateTimes attributes define a clockwise animation that will rotate once.

The ease attribute adds a slight ease to the animation to add some finesse.

```
1  <Motion duration="10" xmlns="fl.motion.*"
   xmlns:geom="flash.geom.*" xmlns:filters="flash.filters.*">
2      <Keyframe index="0" rotateDirection="cw" rotateTimes="1">
3          <tweens>
4              <SimpleEase ease="0.8"/>
5          </tweens>
6      </Keyframe>
7      <Keyframe index="5" x="200" y="200"/>
8  </Motion>
```

The AnimatorExample class starts by loading the XML file previously created. Once the XML file is loaded, the data is cast as (or converted to) XML, a circle is created, and an Animator instance is created with two parameters. The first parameter is the XML that defines the animation; the second is the circle, which the animation will be applied to. Last, the play function is called from the Animator instance, and the animation begins.

TIP  In the following example, the Animator instance needs to be a class property. If it is not, Flash's garbage collector removes the instance before the animation completes.

Animator must be imported to instantiate the Animator class and create the animation.

animator at class scope ensures animations complete before garbage collector removal.

```
1  package
2  {
3      import fl.motion.Animator;
4      import fl.motion.MotionEvent;
5      import flash.display.*;
6      import flash.events.Event;
7      import flash.net.URLLoader;
8      import flash.net.URLRequest;
9
10     public class AnimatorExample extends Sprite
11     {
12         private var animator:Animator;
13
14         public function AnimatorExample():void
15         {
```

The Motion XML file is loaded, and the onAnimationLoaded method is called when the data is available.

A circle is created to use in the animation.

The Animator is constructed from the Motion XML and the DisplayObject used in the animation.

An event can be applied to the animator instance to notify a class method when the animation has ended.

```
16        var animationLoader:URLLoader = new URLLoader();
17        animationLoader.addEventListener(Event.COMPLETE,
   onAnimationLoaded);
18        animationLoader.load(
   new URLRequest("path/file.xml"));
19    }
20
21    private function onAnimationLoaded(e:Event):void
22    {
23        var loader:URLLoader = URLLoader(e.target);
24        var animationXML:XML = new XML(loader.data);
25
26        var circle:Sprite = new Sprite();
27        circle.graphics.beginFill(0x333333);
28        circle.graphics.drawCircle(50, 50, 50);
29        addChild(circle);
30
31        this.animator = new Animator(animationXML,
   circle);
32        this.animator.play();
33        this.animator.addEventListener(
   MotionEvent.MOTION_END, onMotionComplete);
34    }
35
36    private function onMotionComplete(e:MotionEvent):void
37    {
38        trace("onMotionComplete");
39    }
40    }
41 }
```

There are many more new features in ActionScript 3, but now you are armed with an understanding of its essential concepts, so you will quickly pick up any AS3 code that was not covered in this book. You have the core knowledge to build upon, no matter how complex the concept. Have fun with this new knowledge and don't be afraid to make mistakes. Just remember, there is never a wrong way to learn, make the code work with what you know, and you'll improve with experience.

# Index